ENERGY TRANSCENDENCE

A Guide for Living Beyond the Ordinary Range of Perception

by

Dr. Larry Lytle

authorHOUSE®

AuthorHouse™
1663 Liberty Drive, Suite 200
Bloomington, IN 47403
www.authorhouse.com
Phone: 1-800-839-8640

First published by AuthorHouse 11/5/2007

ISBN: 978-1-4343-4416-8 (sc)

Library of Congress Control Number: 2007907790

Printed in the United States of America
Bloomington, Indiana

This book is printed on acid-free paper.

DEDICATION

I dedicate this book *Energy Transcendence* in memory of my mentors; **Jack Schwarz** and **Dr Buddy Frumpker.**

Bless their spirits!

In the memory of Jack Schwarz (deceased 2001) one of the great energy gurus of our times

In memory of Buddy Frumker (deceased2006). Buddy was Jack's student, my friend and a great and thoughtful author.

To all who seek a better understanding of ENERGY and how to transcend the energy of negative experiences into positive energy.

ACKNOWLEDGEMENT

Some Material, including but not limited to chapters 9 and 10, were reproduced from *Mind Map*, with permission of the author, Buddy Frumpker.

CONTENTS

Foreword   xiii

Preface: An Invitation to a Life of Abundance   xv

     A Synthesis of East and West   xvi

     The Mind-body Continuum   xvii

     A Direct Message   xvii

     Renounce and Enjoy   xix

     Restoration of Physical Health   xix

     Framework for Everyone   xix

     The Discovery of Life's Purpose   xx

     A Scientific Method   xxii

     The Test of Increased Abundance   xxii

CHAPTER 1   TRANSCENDENCE

   1.1   What is Transcendence?   1

   1.2   Appropriate and Inappropriate Forces   4

   1.3   Discovering the Direction of Your Life   6

   1.4   Fear and the Law of Equivalent Returns   7

   1.5   Time   10

   1.6   Intent   11

   1.7   The Importance of Intent   13

   1.8   Competence and Spontaneity   16

   1.9   Prayer   16

   1.10   Positive versus Negative   19

   1.11   Learn From Your Mistakes   20

   1.12   You Are the Expert   21

CHAPTER 2   THE STATE OF OUR HEALTH

   2.1   Figures Lie and Liars Figure   23

   2.2   Failure of Alternative Medicine   24

   2.3   Human Genome Project   26

   2.4   Longevity and Diet   27

   2.5   Energy Medicine   28

CHAPTER 3   ENERGY BASICS

3.1	What is Energy?	29
3.2	Sea of Electromagnetic Radiation	30
3.3	Electromagnetic Spectrum	31
3.4	Wave Length	32

CHAPTER 4   UNIVERSAL ENERGY

4.1	What is Universal Energy?	35
4.2	An Alternative Model	36
4.3	The Laws of Thermodynamics	37
4.4	Who, What and Why Are We?	39
4.5	Why then was our physical body created? Why are we here?	40
4.6	Newton's Laws of Motion	41
4.7	Movement toward Evolution and Harmony	43
4.8	Black Hole and Zero Point Field	43
4.9	Primary Perception	44

CHAPTER 5   CREATIVE ENERGY

5.1	Blueprint for Immortality	46
5.2	Where Do Photons Come From?	47
5.3	What is the Casimir Effect – Aether?	48

CHAPTER 6   HUMAN ENERGY

6.1	Homeostasis	50
6.2	The Jack Schwarz Story	52
6.3	This is Not a Miracle	53
6.4	Atoms	54
6.5	Cells	56
6.6	Ph – Potential Hydrogen	57
6.7	Piezoelectric	57
6.8	Redox	58
6.9	Nitric Oxide	58
6.10	New information on cellular communication	59
6.11	Biophotons	60

CHAPTER 7   BRAIN

7.1	Five Brain Waves	62
7.2	Delta Brain Waves	63
7.3	Theta Brain Waves	64
7.4	Alpha Brain Waves	64
7.5	Beta Brain Waves	65
7.6	Gamma Brain Waves	65
7.7	Meditation	67
7.8	Why Meditate?	67
7.9	Practice Counting Your Breath	69

CHAPTER 8   MIND

8.1	The Power of the Total Mind	70
8.2	Abundance through the Universal Mind	71
8.3	Speed of Light	72
8.4	The Conscious Mind	74
8.5	The Subconscious Mind	75
8.6	The Paraconscious Mind	77
8.7	Measuring the Mind's Functions	78
8.8	Two Paraconscious Functions	78
8.9	Action: an Essential Connection	79
8.10	Excitement: Energy in Motion	80
8.11	The Circuit of Self-empowerment	80
8.12	Learning Total Mind Power	82
8.13	Ways the Mind Communicates	83
8.14	Biofeedback	84
8.15	Thought	85

CHAPTER 9   USING PSYCHO-PHYSICAL RE-HERSAL FOR ENERGY TRANSCEN-DENCE

9.1	Introduction to Psycho-Physical Rehearsal	87
9.2	The Basic Steps of Energy Transcendence Using Psycho-Physical Rehearsal	88
9.3	More Power for the Future	89
9.4	Steps for Future Psycho-physical Rehearsal	90

9.5   More Power and Radiance   91
9.6   Thought Patterns and Psycho-Physical Rehearsal   92
9.7   The Experience of Non-attachment   94
9.8   Reaction versus Response   95
9.9   Repetition, Repetition, Repetition   98
9.10 Using Psycho-Physical Rehearsal to Transcend Fear   100
9.11 Facing a Hostile Environment   100
9.12 The Experience of Spontaneity   101
9.13 Access to a Great Source of Information   101
9.14 Plan of Action   105

CHAPTER 10 BREATHING

10.1   Introduction   107
10.2   Level 1—High Breathing   108
10.3   Level 2—Mid-Breathing   109
10.4   Level 3—Low Breathing   109
10.5   Level 4---The Complete Breath   110
10.6   Level 5—Full Breathing   111
10.7   Level 6—Correct Breathing   112
10.8   Breathing Rhythms and States of Consciousness   113
10.9   Breathing Exercises   114
10.10 Beta Breathing   115
10.11 Alpha Breathing   116
10.12 The Alpha-Theta Transfer   116
10.13 Theta Breathing   117
10.14 Delta Breathing   118
10.15 A Combination Exercise   119
10.16 Breathing and Repression of Feelings   120
10.17 The Right Breathing Pattern for You   120
10.18 The Excitement Factor   121
10.19 The Fallacy of Aging   123

CHAPTER 11 PROPRIOCEPTIVE FEEDBACK TO THE BRAIN AND ITS ROLE IN CONTROLLING THE AUTONOMIC NERVOUS SYTSTEM

11.1   What is Proprioception?   125
11.2   Why Haven't I Heard About Proprioception?   126
11.3   Will Result In Reduced Blood Flow to Your Brain   128
11.4   Imbalance between Your Body's Sympathetic (SNS) & Parasympathetic Nervous Systems (PNS)   129

CHAPTER 12 TRANSCENDENCE WITH LOW LEVEL LASERS

12.1   Introduction to Lasers   130
12.2   What Are Lasers?   131
12.3   How Do Low Level Lasers Work?   132
12.4   Why Haven't I Heard About Low Level Lasers?   134
12.5   Where Can I Go To Get Treatment?   135
12.6   Where Can I Go To Learn More About Low Level Lasers?   136

Appendix 1 - Easy Combination Technique   139

References: 141

Other Reading and References: 143

FOREWORD

Energy is everywhere. Everything in and of the universe is energy, including, but not limited to those things you can see, such as, the material things around you and the bodies of all creatures including humans. Energy extends well beyond what you can see and even into the depths of the unknown – the black hole. Energy is before you and around you and in you as you read these lines. It is there waiting to be tapped into and utilized. The most important and misunderstood and misinterpreted energy is thought. For most people it seems nearly impossible not to think. Unfortunately, an estimated 80% of people's thoughts are negative. Negative thoughts are counter productive to mental and physical health and wellbeing as well as longevity of the material body.

Energy Transcendence not only gives you a background in energy but it also gives you answers to pave your road back to a healthier happier YOU. The breathing and meditation exercises may seem hard at first, but keep trying. Once achieved, you will be able to handle and control stress, even though you may not understand the full meaning of the word "stress". A more complete understanding of stress is found by listening to Dr Lytle's *Healing Light DVD* on Proprioception to the Brain

Everyone is unique and will approach a book like this in his or her own way. Here are some suggestions on how you can extract the most from *Energy Transcendence*. The first part of this book is background and is non-interactive; in contrast, the chapters on breathing and psycho-physical rehearsal require your participation. I am a messenger for Jack Schwarz and Buddy Frumker from which much of the knowledge and wisdom in this book is gleaned with embellishment from your author.

If you are like me, you may want to read the table of contents, the preface and chapter 1 on transcendence, and then go directly to the interactive part of the book. Unless you are already a skilled meditator, you may want to try the quick meditation techniques in chapter 7, and then delve more into chapter 9 on psycho-physical rehearsal and chapter 10 to begin practicing your breathing rhythms. For the very busy person, the most important chapter is 12 on Transcendence with low level lasers. Other readers may intuitively and immediately know *Energy Transcendence* is exactly what they have been waiting for and will begin to devour it.

Learning to meditate was a "hard learn" for me until I began the "count the single breath" method explained in chapter 7. Try this method first. If it works for you, it is a quick way to energy transcendence and balance. But to get the most out of meditation it is necessary to go through the book exactly as it's written. In this way, you'll get the background material necessary to understand and benefit from the exercises and meditations.

Begin practicing the exercise as explained in appendix 1 as soon as possible.

Good luck on the wonderful journey that lies before you!

PREFACE:

AN INVITATION TO A LIFE OF ABUNDANCE

We cannot teach people anything; we can only help them discover it within themselves.

-Galileo Galilei

My goal in this book is to present my understanding of the teachings of Jack Schwarz and his student, Buddy Frumpker, and to embellish them with my own "pearls." This wisdom will give you the means for achieving a life of abundance. I realize this is an ambitious goal, however, I know the Jack Schwarz method leads to abundant, radiant lives. Thousands of people have already learned from Jack how to develop vast personal power and internal resources. Their lives have been dramatically changed. My own life is remarkably different today from when I met Buddy Frumpker at the American Society for Physiologic Dentistry. There I began a journey of learning which has been invaluable to me, and I hope, for humankind.

Jack Schwarz was born in Holland in 1924 and immigrated to the United States in 1957. A year later, he established the Aletheia Psycho-Physical Foundation. Aletheia is the Greek word for truth. Aletheia is nonprofit center for education and research in all areas of holistic health. Since Jack's death in 2001, the Foundation has been operated by his wife Lois in Ashland, Oregon.

As a child, Jack realized he had an exceptional ability to control pain and other physiological processes that are thought of as involuntary. He could inflict wounds on himself without feeling pain, and then heal those same wounds within seconds. He could control his heart rate and his body temperature. Jack knew this talent was exceptional only because other people expressed amazement. As he began to investigate the nature of his gift, he learned that his abilities were similar to those practiced by holy men in the yogic and Tibetan Buddhist traditions.

A Synthesis of East and West

Wanting to understand and enhance his talent, Jack studied philosophy, history and religion. He found similar ideas in both eastern and western thought. But he found few, if any, westerners who could do what a highly disciplined yoga or Tibetan monk could do. The reason for this, he eventually concluded, was that people in the west devote all their time to the study of ideas while neglecting the practical application of what they've learned. Consequently, he decided to see whether he could develop a system that would be palatable to the western mind and he included a special emphasis on action and experience. In his synthesis of eastern and western thought, Jack developed a system using one's mind that could be practiced in the context of western society, and which attained new levels of abundance in all areas of life. Buddy Frumpker further elaborated on these principles in his book, *Mind Map*, a 1994 publication now out of print. Jack became well-known in research circles for his ability to control his body processes with his mind. His powers were documented at the Menninger Foundation and the Langley Porter Neuropsychiatric Institute. In one instance for Menninger scientists, Jack pushed a six-inch darning needle into the biceps of his left arm. The needle went through skin, muscle and a vein. After pulling the needle out and letting the wound bleed for fifteen seconds, Jack announced he would stop the bleeding. Two seconds later, the bleeding stopped. Monitoring equipment showed that he was under no unusual stress during this whole exhibition. In fact, all signs indicated he was totally relaxed.

On another occasion, before the Los Angeles County medical and hypnosis associations, Jack picked up burning coals and carried them around in his bare hands for several minutes. When he finally put the coals down, his hand showed no burns or other signs of having been exposed to extreme heat.

The Mind-body Continuum

Jack believed that there is an enormous power surrounding all of us. He called this power the Universal Mind and he described it as a large field of energy and information that fills the universe. This Universal Mind is the intelligence that created the universe and keeps it functioning. The human mind is part of the Universal Mind. When we use our human minds to gain access to it, we can turn universal power into personal power. We can achieve almost anything with this newly acquired ability. We can, as Jack did, control our own physiology—and much more.

Jack felt that part of his mission in this life was to teach others how to achieve the personal power he achieved. He developed programs at Aletheia which were designed to empower others. He also traveled throughout the world demonstrating his abilities and sharing his methods for achieving the miraculous.

This author – not unlike Jack – believes my mission is to "make a difference in humankind," and so, it is that I re-construct and re-write the great work of Buddy Frumpker in, *Mind Map*.

A Direct Message

I have all of Jack Schwarz's publications, including *Human Energy Systems* and I am thrilled to have read them. Jack's books seemed to be speaking directly to the reader, touching on life's trials encountered while searching for the meaning of life. Many have asked the question: What is the purpose of life? Finally after reading *Mind Map*, I found some answers to account for life in a way that made sense to me.

I had built a successful dental practice, specializing in nutrition, bite problems, and head, neck and shoulder pain. I have lectured, and still do, on many of the treatment techniques in these areas and have written *Healing Light* and numerous articles in my field. I could not accept any system that substituted superstition for science. I was looking for a powerful synthesis.

Human Energy Systems and the *Path of Action* offered that synthesis. What Jack described in his books matched my unanswered questions. Jack could read auras. Without hearing a thing from the subject Jack would tell them all about their life and health. He usually was right in everything he said. He quoted from "The Ballad of Reading Gaol," by Oscar Wilde.

"Yet each man kills the thing he loves. .

The coward does it with a kiss,

The brave man does it with a sword!"

Jack explained why each man kills the thing he loves. Jack said that whatever happens to us in life, good or bad, we become attached to it. If we have problems, solving them becomes our focus. We make our problems such a large part of our lives that we have, in effect, fallen in love with our problems–our sicknesses. The same thing happens with our successes. We become so enamored with what we achieve that we want to bask in its glory forever.

These kinds of attachments, he said—whether to problems, successes or both—take us away from our purpose in life, which is to continually move to higher levels of consciousness and awareness. To evolve, we must use our problems and successes as stepping stones instead of becoming so attached to them that we cannot move on. This does not mean we can't pay attention to our problems or glory in our achievements; it means once we have removed an obstacle or enjoyed a success, we cut ourselves free of any attachment and integrate what we have learned into a more powerful self.

To do this requires tremendous courage. Change is what people fear most. Cowards kiss their problems and achievements and remain attached to them, thereby killing the opportunity for growth. Brave individuals cut their attachments so they can move to a higher level of consciousness.

Renounce and Enjoy

To learn how to practice the kind of non-attachment Jack was talking about, you must study and practice *Energy Transcendence*. Mahatma Gandhi may have explained non-attachment best when he responded to a reporter's question when he asked Gandhi to explain in twenty-five words or less the reason he had led such a successful life, one so full of great achievement; Gandhi answered, "Young man, I can indeed tell you what I did to achieve my great successes. But I do not need as many as twenty-five words. I need only three. And those three words are Renounce and Enjoy."

Restoration of Physical Health

For most people to renounce and enjoy they must first deal with their or their family's personal health problems. Jack never diagnosed or treated anyone but he opened doors and pointed them in the right direction. That is what *Energy Transcendence* will do – it will open doors and point you in the right direction. *Energy Transcendence* will not give you all of the answers but it provides a framework for you to begin – to begin to change your ways and to find the right answers from universal energy.

The basics are that your own body already has all of the knowledge and tools it needs to restore health and remain healthy. Healing does not come from outside the body; it's an inside job. By learning how to listen to your body, you, too, can unlock the universal energy needed to heal yourself. In *Energy Transcendence*, you will discover how to use the power of your total mind to transcend and go beyond your problems. You will learn that when you empower your mind and turn your problems over to it, you will overcome them.

Framework for Everyone

Remarkable as his own powers were, Jack's greatest gift was his ability to help others empower themselves. Very few people who possess unusual abilities understand the mechanics of how to teach these abilities. Not only did Jack understand how he achieved his abilities, he also gave us insight to guide others to greatly enlarge their powers. Hundreds of people have gone through the Aletheia program. Some had been told they suffered from incurable health problems when they began to work with Jack. Some were burdened with seemingly unsolvable emotional problems. Jack did not attempt to cure or treat these people or to hand them solutions. Instead, he taught them how to empower themselves, and then tap the more powerful resources available to all.

If you learn this technique, the results will be breathtaking. You literally will become a new person, more powerful and resourceful than ever before. Chronic health problems will disappear and allergies will vanish. One of Jack's students literally got out of her wheel chair and went back to work. If you have emotional problems, you will find the way to resolution via *Energy Transcendence*. One student exclaimed: "for the first time in fifty-eight years, I AM FREE". Another said that with Jack's guidance, she found "the courage to stop doubting." Still another commented, "Instead of making me reliant on him, Jack gave me the tools with which it became possible for me to heal myself." WOW! Isn't that what medicine is all about – to be a teacher rather than a curer?

The Discovery of Life's Purpose

One of my greatest achievements was the discovery of my life's purpose. That is: "To make a difference in human kind".   I realize that when I help others I achieve meaning and abundance for myself.

Writing this and other books and the development of the Q Laser System, is a major part of my life's purpose.

I don't imagine I have to tell you what a magnificent feeling it is to know you are on earth for a reason and that you have the ability to achieve your purpose. Knowing your life's purpose is the starting point for your achievement. Once you understand this – you will get to know yourself. Sounds like a simple task - right? Wrong! Self-knowledge can be the most elusive goal of all.

Each "self" is a distinct and unique entity, precious to the universal intelligence. Most people, because of our training, develop a BIG ego, which bears the responsibility for separating us from each other and the rest of the world. Ego tends to identify you with your physical body and blocks out the underlying, unchanging personal essence that defines each of you. Actually experiencing and getting to know your essence is one of the "highs" of this life.

You may very well be skeptical of what I'm saying here. I'm not asking you to take my claims on faith. You are going to be given a way to test everything. When you follow the programs outlined in *Energy Transcendence*, you'll find they lead you to the abundant life, the overflowing life, the life we all desire and were put on this earth to experience. Such a life can be yours—not for the taking, but for the doing.

The material in this book is both scientific and experiential. That means you actually put it into practice and see for yourself what you can achieve. You put it to work as you go through the interactive chapters. When you use the meditations outlined, your life will change for the better.

You are about to embark on a journey that will change your life. This journey will lead you to fulfill your highest destiny, to live in health and abundance and to soar to heights you never imagined possible. The point of this is bringing the Universal Mind into your everyday life.

The Universal Mind is the power that created the entire universe, including you. Soon you will be using this power routinely. *Energy Transcendence* will impact everything you do, every action you take. You will grow in power and awareness, and you will come to know your life's purpose.

The Universal Mind is everywhere, surrounding you completely and moving within you. Until now you have been severely limited in your ability to perceive the Universal Mind. *Energy Transcendence* will expand your perception. You will learn how to use every part of your mind and to express its power in your life. Through the use of applied active meditation, you will come in contact with the Universal Mind, and incorporate its intelligence into your daily life. The Jack Schwarz psycho/physical rehearsal method has been perfected over twenty-five years of practical application. It has brought health and abundance to thousands. Now you also can be among those who profit from its practice.

A Scientific Method

The *Energy Transcendence* techniques emphasized, including the quick meditation techniques as well as applied active meditation and low level laser have their basis in science. They build on the laws of the universe that human science has discovered and teaches you to move in accordance with these universal laws.

Most of the great discoveries of science have come through the rigorous testing of models called hypotheses. A hypothesis is something not yet proven but assumed to be true for the purposes of further study or investigation. Scientists construct hypotheses in order to predict outcomes. When the predicted outcomes consistently occur, the hypothesis is said to be scientifically valid.

As you proceed through this book, you will use meditation to devise plans of action for your daily life. The consistent, predictable success you achieve through your actions will scientifically validate the process. You can never know truth by reading about it. The only way to know truth is to experience it.

The Test of Increased Abundance

The predictable outcome of understanding energy basics, low level laser therapy, universal and human energy and using meditation to access your energy will be increased abundance and peace in your life. You will actually begin to achieve abundance for yourself as you apply meditations to your life. When each meditation consistently brings you abundance, you will have proven its validity. Each meditation will help you to build within yourself that knowledge and those powers that will bring you more abundance.

Abundance is an overflowing fullness, and richness in all areas of your life. Our culture teaches us to think about abundance only in the material sense. Obviously, financial and physical health are important aspects of an abundant life, but true health is complete social, mental, physical, dental, and spiritual well being – not just the absence of disease. Balancing the human and universal energy offers you abundance of emotional, mental and spiritual riches. A life of abundance is a life with direction and purpose. Discovering your life's purpose and living it is what the late Joseph Campbell so beautifully called, "living your bliss." Living your bliss is living abundantly.

Applied active meditation is not something you sit in a corner and do for an hour each day. It is a method of living your life so that each day adds to your wisdom, power and abundance. It is a daily program which transcends the energy expended in anger, fear, guilt, envy, worry, and the rest of these destructive cousins into achieving well being, happiness and health. This is accomplished by transcending negative energy into positive energy.

Meditation leads to immediate action in your everyday life. Your life is the testing laboratory for the effectiveness of the meditation method. As you test each meditation and prove the process valid, your life will become continually more exciting, with each day offering new opportunities. Abundance will become a predictable part of your life.

Through *Energy Transcendence* you will learn:

1. The basics of energy

2. How to use all the functions of your mind

3. How to greatly increase the power of your mind

4. How to use your total mind power in daily life to achieve abundance

5. And finally, how to use the Q Laser system, a low level laser system that restores energy in the form of electrons, back to the injured or sick cell.

This book is arranged to encourage you to continue on the path of applied active meditation aided by Q Laser therapy so you will see the rewards right away. Seeing immediate rewards, such as pain control, makes it easier to transcend negative into positive. Remember, the first rewards are mere glimpses of the vast power you are beginning to tap into. The best is always yet to come

I increased my personal power by quantum amounts. Not only did I begin to achieve more and more of my life goals, but success became predictable, almost inevitable. And as I bubbled over with the joy of such success, I had an irresistible urge to share the way to achieve it. With *Energy Transcendence* as your guide, you can construct and scientifically prove your own program. Use it, live it and watch in wonder as it changes your life.

May your journey be as miraculous as mine!

Chapter 1

TRANSCENDENCE

We may well go to the moon, but that's not very far: the greatest distance we have to cover still lies within us.
Charles de Gaulle, French statesman 1890-1970

1.1   What is Transcendence?

Transcendence is the state of being or existing above and beyond the limits of material experiences. Transcending from negative to positive is important in living a healthy happy life.

It is also an important concept in the applied active meditation program. In transcendence, you look for the appropriate force that is the opposite of an inappropriate force. Then you replace the negative with the positive. Transcendence is one of the most powerful tools available to you. You do not correct what is inappropriate, you replace it. When you replace anything inappropriate with what is appropriate, you become more powerful.

Transcendence is developing within yourself the power and wisdom to replace whatever in your life is undesirable and inappropriate with that which is exciting, desirable and appropriate. Through transcendence, almost every problem in your life becomes an opportunity to increase your own personal power.

It sometimes seems the reason life has so many problems is to give us multiple chances to expand and evolve. Every time you transcend a problem rather than merely solving it, you increase awareness.

For example, suppose someone takes an unfair business advantage of you. You can become angry, try to fight back and hurt the individual. And even if you win—what do you win? Instead you can transcend this situation. You can set up a business plan that will increase your personal wealth by far more than you lost.

Supposing you have an argument with a loved one, you can stay angry or respond by writing a love letter or note and set up a wonderful dinner with the person you care about. By handling it this way, you transcend the problem and add to your knowledge in a way that builds your abilities and powers. In both examples, by transcending the situation rather than reacting to it, you have gained resources you did not previously have.

What is the difference between solving problems and transcending them? Solving problems is a function of the conscious mind. To rectify a problem, you must concentrate on it. And by concentrating and putting it in the forefront of your mind, you are likely to attract more of the same. If you just solve the problem, you are the same person who had that problem to begin with. You have not evolved or changed. When the problem reoccurs, as it most likely will, you will know the solution; you will apply it and fix the problem again and again and again. But you are stuck. You have not transcended the problem. You have only temporarily fixed it.

Almost all our education has trained us to focus on and identify with our problems, virtually assuring that we will spend our lives solving the same problems over and over and over again. To step off this treadmill, remember that any problem you face is the direct result of the specific forces that produced it. Identifying the forces that are influencing you is a function of your total mind: conscious, subconscious and paraconscious.

In transcendence, you concentrate on pulling more intelligence from the Universal Mind into the field of your awareness, thus expanding it. You do not focus on the particular problem. For instance, suppose you have a particular health problem – perhaps an enlarged prostate gland. Learn not to focus on that problem, rather identify the forces that had your physical self out of balance and concentrate on restoring the functions of your entire body. Rather than treating symptoms, you correct causes. This process will leave you with a stronger and better body. It will transform you into more powerful and resourceful person.

When you practice transcendence you will always experience this same kind of growth. When you encounter problems, practice transcendence and you will not be the same person afterward. You will have evolved. When you apply the opposite force to the one that produced the problem, you not only solve the problem, you also add a positive force to your energy field. This force is now yours to call on whenever you need it.

Transcendence is possible because the universe is bipolar. It is made-up of opposite energies—positive and negative. When positive and negative poles are connected by a conductor, energy flows. When warm air from the south moves northward and cold air from the north moves southward, they meet to create an incredibly strong flow of energy called the jet stream.

In your life, the joining of a negative experience with its opposite positive can also create tremendous energy as powerful as a jet stream and it will propel you through life. Negative experiences by themselves impede or even stop the flow of universal creative energy through you. Positive experiences by themselves improve your energy flow somewhat. But the greatest power of all comes from joined polarities. A life restricted to positive experiences will be a less radiant life than one in which positive and negative are joined. Every time you connect a negative experience to a positive one and turn on the "current" by taking action, you create within yourself an enormous flow of creative energy.

The key point is that a negative experience remains negative only as long as it is not joined to a positive experience. Thus the loss of function and the resultant miseries arising from negative experiences are not from the experiences themselves. Rather, they emanate from the failure to link those negative experiences to matching positives; in every new linkage you achieve the potential to create enormous new powers within yourself. That is transcendence—taking individual negative experiences, linking them to positive experiences, and creating within your body, mind and soul new and greater power than ever existed before.

1.2   Appropriate and Inappropriate Forces

Appropriate forces are those forces pushing toward success and growth. The forces keeping you back are inappropriate. Appropriate forces are excitement, zest, desire, faith, confidence, high self-esteem, etc. Inappropriate forces are fear, hate, bitterness, anger, low self-esteem, self-righteousness, etc. When you actually write down and record the forces operating in your life, you immediately increase greatly the power of the appropriate ones and, at the same time, dramatically decrease the power of those that are inappropriate.

In listing appropriate and inappropriate forces, you need to join a negative with a positive – never dwell on the negative.

This input from your conscious mind is built on the experiences of your daily life and based on logical verification. It helps to write and describe your thoughts prior to and during your meditation. First write the thoughts that helped the process proceed and flow. Examples of these would be images of the target you have set or the action you would like to take.

Write about what you feel emotionally and also what you feel inside your body. What areas feel strong? Where do you experience a powerful energy flow? What parts of you feel hot? Which parts of you feel vibrant and healthy? Describe as much as you can about your emotions and your feelings. The greater your awareness of these things, the greater is your power to be in control of your life.

Knowing comes only from experience. Knowing occurs when your paraconscious mind brings intelligence from the Universal Mind into your subconscious mind which, in turn, integrates this new information with all the input that has preceded it. The subconscious mind then presents new and more powerful plans of action to your conscious mind, and your conscious mind puts these plans to work in your daily life. The result is the circuit of self-empowerment, one of the most powerful processes available to any human being.

By the act of writing you are putting intelligence from the Universal Mind to work in your daily life. Your perspective on the meditation you have just completed is dramatically new because of the knowledge your subconscious mind has processed and fed into a plan of action. You will be able to identify your plan and to act on it.

Once you have listed all the positive forces that were at work during your meditation, go back and describe the inhibiting forces, those that seemed to hinder the motion of the process. The thoughts holding you back will be fairly obvious. They appear as fears, doubts and feelings of incompetence. Self-righteous thoughts and judgments of other people are inappropriate forces, as are any thoughts that place you apart from other people and in competition with them.

Make a note of those feelings that are interfering. What parts of your body feel funny? Where do you sense a weak energy flow: your stomach, libido or sexual energy? What areas are cold: your hands, feet or head? Which parts of you feel dull and sick? What emotions and feelings do you experience with each action in your meditation assessment?

Finally, describe any inappropriate knowledge that you have. If, for example, you devise a plan that is aimed at taking advantage of other people or winning out over others, you may want to repeat the exercise. Something has broken your circuit of self-empowerment somewhere along the line.

Virtually everyone encounters problems and frustrations. Sometimes you suffer severely. You have been taught to look at problems as undesirable and even horrible. However, as many others have already learned, through their problems they achieved a higher state. You, too, can use them to establish circuits of self-empowerment and hence increase your personal power and energy.

The moment you observe an action from your day and deem it inappropriate, you have devalued that action. You have reduced its value. You are no longer emotionally attached to it. As soon as you devalue an action, you free the energy that was attached to it. As long as you concentrate on inappropriate actions, your energy is invested in them and you cannot use it creatively. With energy attached to what is inappropriate for you, you keep repeating your mistakes. Remember like thoughts attract like thoughts. Devaluing an inappropriate action frees energy for transformation into something that will enhance your life.

Think about the negatives to which you give value and attach energy. If you concentrate on how dumb, inadequate or bad you were in certain situations, you are giving value to those qualities. You are attaching energy to them. The price you pay for tying up your energy in these negatives is tremendous. Just acknowledging the action and then making the decision to get on with life is enough. Do not pass negative judgment on yourself. Love yourself and merely deem the action inappropriate, and receive instructions from the Universal Mind for transcending that action. You free energy for use in increasing your personal power. You attach that energy to appropriate actions, and you move to a higher level of existence. Energy attached to appropriate actions is creative. It is in harmony with the Universal Mind.

1.3   Discovering the Direction of Your Life

To complete the meditation, you must take the action suggested to you by the Universal Mind. Write and describe this action in detail. Was it spontaneous? How immediate was it? As a result of the action, what do you now know?

Each entry will be a record of the circuit of self-empowerment. Your journal makes you active in the flow of your life. You can read it and see yourself unfold. The essence of your life lies not in the things happening to you, but in the relationship you establish between the Universal Mind and those events. As you enlarge your awareness and broaden your perspective, you will establish a closer relationship between the Universal Mind and what goes on in your daily life. You will discover abilities you didn't know you had and be brought face to face with the meaning of your existence. You will discover your life has, indeed, been going somewhere—however blind you have been to its direction.

No matter how much success you achieve through the methods described in this book, you can always achieve more. Success is not about competing and winning or about amassing material possessions only. Success is completing a meditation and coming out of it with another bit of intelligence from the Universal Mind added to your life. Success in these terms is never a stopping place. The journey doesn't end. You will not collect more of the same material goods. Rather, you will achieve your desires and discover enticing opportunities for greater personal growth. You will continually achieve new heights. The scaling of one peak allows you to view another, higher one.

This sets the stage for your next, even more transformational circuit of self-empowerment. Your life becomes a constant flow.

The purpose of your temporary physical life is to bring as much intelligence from the Universal Mind to your eternal self as you can.

1.4   Fear and the Law of Equivalent Returns

With each addition of power, the likelihood of attracting more power increases. This is the universal law of harmony in action. The law of harmony says that in the non-material world, the eternal world, like attracts like. In the material world unlike poles attract each other. So thoughts, which are non-material, attract similar thoughts and lead to actions that are in harmony with them.

A particular part of the law of harmony is the law of equivalent returns. This says that whatever you concentrate on and focus your attention on, you are in harmony with, and you will achieve. If you concentrate and focus on success that is what you will achieve; if you concentrate and focus on what you fear, likewise that is what you will attract.

The major reason there is so much misery and failure in the world is that the majority of people spend their lives concentrating on problems and keeping track of time. The end result is the world has more problems and never enough time to solve them. The law of equivalent returns tells why you achieve whatever you concentrate on. If the focus is on problems, you will have more problems—even if you appear to solve an immediate problem – more will follow.

For example, when our governments concentrate on fighting crime, as the present history dramatically shows, the result is – there is more crime. When our crippled medical model fights disease, as today's staggering medical bills and mounting suffering confirms, this results in more diseases. All this is predictable by the law of universal harmony and its equivalent returns.

If, instead of concentrating on problems or on what is wrong in their lives, people would concentrate on what they want, what they wish to achieve, they would make progress. For example, when people are economically down and out, if they concentrated on abundance instead of on lack, they would achieve abundance. If, instead of concentrating on defeating racism, we concentrated on achieving brotherhood, there would be a dramatic drop in bigotry. If, rather than focusing on fighting crime and building costly jails, harmony and mutual assistance were stressed, we would have little crime. If, instead of combating drugs, we put our efforts into encouraging lives of joy and quality, the drug problem would disappear. If, instead of battling disease, we concentrated on health, the incidence of disease would dramatically decrease.

The law of equivalent returns tells why a positive mental attitude is so powerful and a negative one so destructive. With a positive mental attitude, your brain focuses on and chooses positive stimuli and ideas. You seem to attract success. In reality, you are choosing success. When your conscious-subconscious mind believes that only success will come your way from the barrage of stimuli it selects, then you will have success.

Since your brain chooses to acknowledge predominantly those stimuli that reinforce your belief systems, what you believe is of crucial importance. And even more crucial is the degree to which you believe. In other words, your mind must be totally filled with whatever you want to attract or you will probably not realize your goals. Even a few fears or doubts remaining in your mind can block the achievement of your desires.

As a human being, you have the freedom to place into your mind whatever you choose. Once you have installed a belief system, however, your freedom is severely restricted. The conscious mind will act according to the resident belief system. The beliefs lodged in your mind determine what you will perceive and what actions you will take.

Fear is the biggest obstacle to happiness and wellness. The thoughts holding you back are not always easy to identify. These fears appear as doubts and feelings of incompetence. Fear truly limits wellness; Fear of sickness, fear of failure and embarrassment, fear of letting your family down, and fear of death are our biggest obstacles. Death is the second worst fear - the worst fear is fear of disability. Fear that you will become sick or injured and unable to do the things you want and need to do for yourself and your family and that you will need someone else care for you is the biggest fear. To be healthy and happy you must learn to transcend these fears.

Fear, expectations, and beliefs can block healing. Diagnosis, in and of itself, may instill more fear than your mind and immune system can handle. Diagnosis puts your mind to work in negative ways. Just think, suppose you get a diagnosis of AIDS and it is wrong; what chance do you think you have of surviving? Here is a bit of advice: never have any tests or diagnosis unless you have already decided how you will deal with the results, either positive or negative. A plus for today's medicine is that if you have been in an accident, western surgeons are the best in the world at putting you back together. However, if you have a degenerative disease, surgery may be of little value and in the long run may make things worse by suppressing the immune system and blocking the flow of healing energy.

It is easy to say "don't be afraid", but many of the fears are hidden fears introduced by grandparents, parents, schools, churches, governments and, most of all, those that you trust such as your doctors and close friends. This environment constitutes beliefs, which, in the long run, constitute your fears. Let go of those fears that are pulling you into disease and distress.

In this day of degenerative disease, diagnosis may be the worst thing you can have done. Diagnosis breeds fear and fear suppresses the immune system causing disease. There is a big word for this called "psychoneuroendocrineimmunology." When the word is broken down, it makes more sense – psycho means thought – neuro means the nervous systems – endocrine refers to the glandular system and immunology is the body's defense system. So how one thinks <u>does</u> affect health and wellness.

1.5   Time

Time is as the mind thinks it is. In disease it can be your enemy, i.e. how long do I have doc? How long will this take to heal? How bad is it? The "fear" questions go on and on and in many cases prove to be true. I predict that someday soon, some aggressive attorney will bring a law suit – possibly even charging the doctor with a crime, when he/she predicts that you, their patient, only have six months to live. Time is not in the hands of your doctor and predictions may accelerate the disease, therefore the prediction will come true.

As an example of the effects time can have, twelve miners were trapped in a UK mine accident. The engineers knew the size of the room and that only about 12 hours of oxygen were available. They informed the foreman that they were drilling a hole to force in oxygen but that it would take 24 hours. The foreman, the only man with a watch, decided he would give hope to his crew, so he called out the time every hour – only he extended it to 2 hours. So when one hour had passed he did not say anything. When two hours passed, he told his crew it had been one hour. When four hours passed, he told them it had been two hours and so on. When they broke through with the oxygen at 23 ½ hours all the men were alive except the foreman – the man with the watch. The foreman knew there was not enough oxygen for them to survive and therefore, he died, but the rest of the crew did not know the time and they lived. Be careful how you interpret time.

I am sure all of you have awakened and looked at the clock, decided to catch a few extra winks and gone back to sleep going into the dream state. The dream seemed to cover hours or even days, only to wake up and realize you had only been asleep for a few minutes. Now, think how time when coupled with diagnosis affects our health – this injury will take 6 months to heal – this medicine will take 4 hours to work – cancer is diagnosed and your doctor says you have 6 months to live, or that your family, your mother, father and siblings have all died in their 60s. What are your chances of living longer?

1.6   Intent

Intent has a great deal to do with your health and wellbeing. Dr. William Tiller, a man that someday may receive the Nobel Prize for his work, is in the process of rewriting Einstein's Quantum Theory. In one of Tiller's studies, he placed four experienced meditators in a room with a controlled environment along with two beakers of pure water. An experienced meditator is someone who can immediately put his/her mind in neutral and not think. They have the ability, usually through breathing rhythms, to put their brain waves in alpha or even delta. Pure water has a neutral Ph of 7. The meditators intent was to change the Ph of one beaker from neutral, a Ph of 7, to an acid Ph of 6 and leave the other beaker unchanged. They did just that. Then the mediators were asked to change the acidic Ph of

6 to an alkaline Ph of 8, and that happened. At this point one has to wonder what role all this has on our body's Ph.

In another experiment Tiller asked his meditators to add an enzyme to one beaker and they were able to do that. Intent is very powerful. Tiller's work brings into question every research project ever done because the intent of the researcher will come through in the results of the experiment. Intention or expectation of the experimenter may influence the outcome of studies. Marilyn Schlitz in her article, *Intentional Healing,* explores research documenting that results follow the experimenter's intention. It is scary to think that our medical model is based upon intention of the researchers, drug companies, and controlled thinking at the University levels[1]. There are different forms of intention. "Intolerant intention leads to conflict and even wars. Subtle, direct or compassionate intention toward another, with love, peace, joy, and wholeness is the most powerful intention and can affect the well-being of others, even the entire world."

The intent of visualization and guided imagery has been shown to be successful in controlling cancer. Visualizing wellness and a desired future state of health with some emotional oomph behind it works not only in healing but in mind/body self-regulation. Cancer research shows that there are three main things involved in overcoming cancer: (1) Do you want to live; (2) Do you have a health care provider that supports your philosophy and (3) Does your family or third party support you and your chosen health care provider's choice of treatment? When all three of these are present, cancer recovery will be better regardless of the treatment. Studies have shown that guided imagery and music intervention reduce anxiety. Another study showed that guided imagery, visualization and journaling resulted in a significant reduction in irritable bowel syndrome which is more prevalent than diabetes in the US.[2]

It seems clear that energy healing must be the medicine of the future. Jerry E. Wesch, in an article entitled, *Energy Healing* published in *Subtle Energies & Energy Medicine* states: "People move on in their spiritual evolution by developing, a new wider Story, leaving behind the limits of their Old Story of the Universe."[3] For years electromagnetism was in favor to explain one's intention on the well-being of another. Now that we understand non-local energy, electromagnetism is falling from favor. There is this unique Universal energy that cannot be seen or identified that can be directed by human intention and in the future will be known as Energy Medicine or Subtle Energy. Energy Medicine works best when you let go of, or significantly modify your previous beliefs about conventional medicine---leaving room for an expanded understanding of our self-responsibility. In a Russian study 5 cages of 10 mice each were randomly assigned to 4 healers with one cage as a control. The healers treated their mice and then the mice were irradiated with a fatal dose of ionizing radiation. Within 19 days all the control mice were dead. Seventy five percent of the energy treated mice were fine. The cage of mice with the best survival rate (90%), were treated from a distance of 800 kilometers, proving that healing is a non-local energy phenomena and distance does not matter.

1.7   The Importance of Intent

The nature of your intent for every psycho-physical rehearsal is paramount. By intent I mean your reason for doing the exercise. Are you doing it to increase your own competence, to raise your own level of consciousness, or are you doing it to beat someone else? For instance, perhaps I want to do something better because I'm embarrassed when you outperform me in public. I am jealous of you. I have some envy. I may even be spiteful. Rather than being in competition with myself, being interested in improving myself, my intent is to be in competition with you so I will look better than you. I might succeed and actually outdo you, but I still have my envy, spite and jealousy. Therefore I will have improved in a particular situation, but I will not have transcended the negative emotions that led me to seek that improvement in the first place. I will always encounter people who can do certain things better than I and all over again I will feel envy, spite and jealousy.

If, however, my intent is to transcend my envy, spite and jealousy, then when I add intelligence from the Universal Mind to myself, I become more powerful. I will have proper actions to take. I will have removed the envy, spite and jealousy not by trying to lessen some one else's power, but by increasing my power until I am completely non-attached to your feelings. As long as my energy is attached to the envy, spite and jealousy, it is not free for me to use. Once I obtain sufficient intelligence and power to free the energy bound by these emotions, then I can apply that energy to any area of my life that I choose.

When your intent is to experience the bipolar reality of each inappropriate occurrence in your life, you will see the appropriate vision with which to replace it. When you replace your inappropriate experience with the appropriate vision from your bipolar experience, you have created a wiser and more powerful you.

Another very important reason for evaluating your intent is to make sure whether at this time you should be doing what you are doing in your psycho-physical rehearsal. If you keep rehearsing and rehearsing and what you experience does not give you excitement and pleasure and joy, you are doing an inappropriate psycho-physical rehearsal. Suppose you want to do a painting, but every time you rehearse it, you feel uncomfortable and feel no excitement. Then you have to ask yourself if you really want to do that painting. The uncomfortable feeling and lack of excitement are telling you that you do not want to paint. The lack of excitement tells you, for whatever reason, your energy is not in motion and flowing. Under these conditions, whatever you do in the psycho-physical rehearsal or in real life will fail! When your psycho-physical rehearsal shows you that you are not yet ready to do something, put that goal aside for a time. Look for the fears, doubts and other negative emotions to which you are attached. Work on becoming non-attached. And work on building your personal power in all ways.

If you are getting ready to perform a specific event or feat and you aim your psycho-physical rehearsal at it, your intent must not be to have control over the one situation but rather to learn to have control over every situation. Therefore if your psycho-physical rehearsal is on a business meeting you are about to have, your desire should go beyond having a successful meeting to learning the process of psycho-physical rehearsal so you can empower yourself to face any situation.

You begin the actual psycho-physical rehearsal by establishing a specific goal. If your goal is to have a successful business meeting, then your paraconscious mind knows to get and bring to you the intelligence that you will need for your meeting. A specific goal gives you a target and the raw material you will use to begin your progress. You need not, however, limit what you achieve during your psycho-physical rehearsal to a specific goal. With input from the Universal Mind, you may achieve a result far beyond your original target, or you may achieve more than one goal. The goal is just the bait by which you get the psycho-physical rehearsal going. The Universal Mind and the bipolar vision you respond to will determine how far you can go during one psycho-physical rehearsal.

The set of circumstances that you work with in your psycho- physical rehearsal should be as close to reality as possible. If one of the people attending your business meeting is very abusive and disruptive, to portray him as kind and cooperative would turn the psycho-physical rehearsal into a mockery. Your intent must be to represent the situation of the psycho-physical rehearsal to your paraconscious as accurately as possible.

Set up the environment of the meeting and become familiar with it. As you explore the environment, you will discover those factors that are interfering with your performance and those that are supporting you. Keep going back to the environment until you have overcome all the interference and are relaxed and in control. Now start into the actual meeting.

At your last business meeting, you were not successful. You felt incompetent to handle many of the problems that arose. For this meeting, first do a cosmic review of the last meeting. Let your paraconscious experience the situation in which you did so poorly. Let your paraconscious show you the bipolar picture. You will see an appropriate vision that achieves what your previous actions failed to achieve. Repeat that disastrous meeting as often as needed. With each repeat, you will become more relaxed and non-attached. You will finally experience yourself competently handling the meeting.

Immediately put your new power into use by rehearsing the upcoming meeting. Become familiar with how it really feels to have this meeting. With each rehearsal, you will make new discoveries and develop new powers. As you put these powers into action in your rehearsal, you'll feel more and more competent. You will learn how success feels.

1.8   Competence and Spontaneity

When, by doing the psycho-physical rehearsal, you come to know you are competent, your doubts and fears will dissolve—your faith, power and excitement will increase—and you will take action spontaneously. Once you act spontaneously and the results prove your competence, you will be even more willing to go immediately with the new input from your paraconscious. The upward spiral will begin. Spontaneous action turns universal intelligence into personal intelligence. The ability to act spontaneously grows out of feelings of self-worth. Competence fuels those feelings. The more able you are, the more worthy you will feel, and the more spontaneously you will act. This spontaneity will increase your power, giving you even more competence and self-worth.

No matter what situation you rehearse, you are not training yourself just for that situation. You are training yourself to become competent in whatever comes along so you can have spontaneous articulation and action. With each psycho-physical rehearsal, you have a marvelous opportunity to experience and become aware of all those hidden things that prevent you from becoming competent.

1.9   Prayer

What about prayer? Is it just a form of subtle energy? Is there such a thing as negative prayer? When the National Institute of Health formed the Complimentary Alternative Medicine division, it began to provide funding for research into various subtle energy projects. One area that had not been researched was prayer. Repeatedly research demonstrates what advocates of prayer have said for centuries – prayer works - at least some of the time. But let me point out that the black plague, one of the mankind's worst disasters, happened during the Christian era in the 13th century when tens of thousands prayed for their loved ones and still watched them die. Again, in the flu epidemic of 1918 tens of thousands died even though they were prayed for. The answer given when prayer did not seem to work was "they have gone to a better place." Since prayer is just energy, is it possible that those praying were praying in the wrong way – with the wrong thoughts or the wrong words?

Research shows that there is such a thing as negative prayer. Research published in *IONS,* September/November 2006 issue of *SHIFT, Can Science Study Prayer,* reports that Dr Herbert Benson, Harvard School of Medicine, and author of the *Relaxation Response,* did a research project on prayer. His study on a group of cardiac patients that did not know they received distant prayer showed no improvement after the prayer. More importantly, the group that knew they were being prayed for was significantly worse than the control group. How can that be?

Another research project, the MANTRA study, done by Dr. Mitchell Frucoff and colleagues at Duke University Medical School, sponsored by IONS showed no results for cardiac patients who were prayed for. In yet another study by Dr. John Austin, California Pacific Medical Center, showed distant prayer had no effect on AIDS patients.

I suggest it is the words used in the prayer that may be the reason for prayer failing. Negative words or thoughts, whether they are through prayer from a loved one or from a caring person from a distance, or by the fearful sick person themselves, reduce the number and coherence of cellular biophoton production and reduce cell to cell communication. The words or thoughts used in the prayer are more important than the act of praying. During prayer, never give power to the disease or disorder by mentioning it. Use positive rather than negative thoughts or words. Example: <u>Do not think</u> or say in your prayers. Please God, cure my mother of this dreaded cancer. A positive prayer is better and more powerful. There is a thin line between intent, prayer, repeating a mantra, healing music or just plain positive thinking.

The following story exemplifies negative prayer. In a small Midwestern town, a man rented a building with the proper zoning and opened a bar right across the street from a Baptist church. The Baptist minister mobilized his congregation and began praying that the bar would close down. Much to the glee of the minister and his congregation, a lightening strike hit the bar and burned it to the ground. The minister commented; "God works in mysterious ways." The bar owner sued the church on the grounds that the church was responsible for the demise of his building and business. The church vehemently denied all responsibility either through direct or indirect actions or means. At the hearing the judge commented; "I don't know how I am going to decide this case but it appears that the bar owner believes in prayer and the minister and his congregation doesn't."

Several years ago when I was regaining my health after being "diagnosed" with heart problems, I wrote the following prayer and repeated it as a song during my exercise regime.

"When the Sun comes up in the East and I see its golden glow,

I know I'm getting better today. I'm getting better, I'm getting better – I'm getting better.

When the Sun is at high noon – I know that - soon I will be better in each and every way. I'm getting better – I'm getting better – I'm getting better.

When the Sun sets down behind the cloud – I'm going to shout right out loud – I am better today – I'm getting better – I'm getting better – I'm getting better!

When the lights twinkle on the square – I am playing – I am dancing – I am laughing. I know that soon I will be better – better in each and every way – I am getting better – I am getting better

And when I lay my head down to sleep and I reflect on a beautiful day – I must say – I'm better in each and every way – I'm getting better – I'm getting better – I'm getting better – TODAY in each and every way – I'm getting better today."

Again I point out that a low powered resonating laser delivers photons and thus electrons back to the cells of the organism just as can be done by positive prayer – they work synergistically.

1.10 Positive versus Negative

There have been many studies done over the years on positive versus negative thinking, many of them in the field of athletics or success in business. Since a thought is just a little squiggly sine wave that can be everywhere at once, positive or negative thinking is not much different than positive or negative prayer. Carnegie Melon Research Centers in a December 2005 press release states "there is a growing field of evidence that positive emotions such as happiness, energetic, full of pep, vigorous people" are healthier and live longer. It is surprising to me that we need research to prove what should be common sense.

It is known that positive thoughts and reactions introduced into the "field" of the person produce an increase in the quantity and quality (coherence) of photons (light) emitted by the cells. It is just the opposite when the reaction or thought is negative. There is a decrease in photon emissions from the cells.

The principle of Homeopathic has been around for many years. German physician, Samuel Hahnemann, developed Homeopathy over 200 years ago, and emphasized that health is a dynamic process of freedom at every level of being. Hahnemann wrote that all disease begins as a "mistunement" at the spiritual level and ultimately manifests at the physical level.

Everything has its own frequency, including microbes and diseased tissue, so it makes good sense to heal with like frequencies. The idea of like heals like is an old philosophy that is being given renewed emphasis. In the 1930s, Royal Rife, studied thousands of microbes, diseased cells, tissues and organs and published frequencies to combat these disorders. His work was mostly done under his famous microscope but when he tried to develop a generator to deliver these frequencies back into the body, he was not very successful. You will learn later how you can have these frequencies programmed into low level lasers for delivering them into the body.

A good source of Rife's work and his applied frequencies are found in the book published by Nina Silvers *"Rife Frequencies."*

1.11 Learn From Your Mistakes

You can use your total mind power to transcend problems. Almost every negative experience offers you the opportunity to connect to a positive and by so doing to increase your personal power. When you link the negatives of the pain and suffering of your daily life to the positives of success and happiness brought to you from the Universal Mind, you create an energy within you that gives you the insight and power to achieve more success and happiness than you could have achieved without this linkage. Once you complete the circuit of self-empowerment, the additional power is yours to use for the rest of your life.

The concept of transcendence has three important parts. First, you must understand the significance and potential of all experiences. Second, you must find a way to join earthly negative experience to its opposite positive in the Universal Mind. The most effective process for doing this is meditation. Third, you must express the action suggested by the Universal Mind in your daily life. It is the expression of the positive action from the Universal Mind that allows your life current to flow.

There are several important first steps toward transcendence and total mind power:

1. Get to know your present self. There is an ancient Hawaiian healing process known as "ho'oponopono" which places total responsibility on you – meaning you are responsible for what you think and do, not what someone else does wrong. Doctors of all disciplines, conventional western doctors, dentists, naturopaths, chiropractors, psychiatrists and all of those that want to help human kind with prevention – energy – nutritional - orthomolecular and homeopathy should first heal themselves before they can heal others. In order to heal anyone, you first must heal yourself. You do that by saying to yourself over and over again – I am sorry – I love you. That is what ho'oponopono means – to love your self. By loving yourself you can rid yourself of the fears and negative thoughts holding you back.

2. You can learn to use your paraconscious mind to tune into the Universal Mind and bring it to yourself. Once you get input from the paraconscious to work in your life, you will have the key to transforming universal power into personal power, and you will be on your way to achieving everything you want.

1.12 You Are the Expert

Adapting processes and methods to your own needs is harder than you realize. It takes courage and responsibility. You have been conditioned to rely on experts for most of what you do in your life. This need for outside authority is deeply rooted in your conscious mind. The first step in preparing for self-awareness is to loosen the rigid control your conscious mind programming exerts. Look to your teachers and experts only for guidance. Look within yourself for the power to achieve. Love yourself.

Become aware of yourself. Pause to ask these questions at each experience: What do I think? What do I feel? What have I learned? What do I now know? Become aware of your emotions, of your existing belief systems, of your desires and fears. Become aware of any feelings and sensations in your body. Face yourself in the mirror and keep reminding yourself that you are sorry for any thing you have done wrong to yourself and to others and that you have forgiven yourself. Repeat over and over again "I LOVE ME."

Chapter 2

THE STATE OF OUR HEALTH

Our lives are shaped not as much by our experiences, as by our expectations
-George Bernard Shaw

2.1   Figures Lie and Liars Figure

You have all heard the statement "figures lie and liars figure." I will quote some statistics with which you may not agree or you may find fault with their accuracy. My intentions are not in any way designed to mislead you or to introduce more fear, but to get you to think. In America we have been brainwashed into believing we are and have the best of everything – including medicine. We have been led by the pharmaceutical companies, insurance companies, the American Hospital Association, the American Medical Association, the American Dental Association, the American Nursing Home Association, multiple chiropractic and naturopathic doctors associations and our government to "just trust us" and turn your health care over to us. We live in a country with a failing health care system that is strongly supported by professional organizations, big corporations and the American Bar Association, and many of its ambulance chasing scurrilous lawyers.

Michael Moore in his 2007 movie *Sicko* places most of the blame for our poor quality and expensive medicine on big insurance companies and the drug industry, but this is not entirely so. The blame for a failed system goes far beyond that. Rather than single out two or three problems with health care in America, it can better be summed up by greed and ego of the insurance industry, doctors and attorneys plus the fact that Americans have not taken responsibility for their own health. Sickness, disability and death many times seem to be someone else's fault and our system encourages people to look outside of themselves for help.

2.2   Failure of Alternative Medicine

For the past 25 years, complementary, alternative, preventive or integrative splinter groups of medicine have entered into health care with high hopes that these uncoordinated groups, each by themselves, can make a difference – to change the failed orthodox, conventional, western medicine model for health care. It has been the goal of the integrative medical community to educate people to use other methods in place of, or along with, orthodox, conventional or allopathic medicine. That goal has been achieved. In 2006 over 50% of the 300 million US residents used some type of integrative, complementary or alternative medicine and at the same time, our population got sicker and died faster. The integrative medical community is very fragmented – each thinking and promoting that they have found the answer – the miracle new vitamin – the magic new technique, but very few of these newer integrative medical groups pay any attention to or base their philosophy and techniques on energy medicine.

Regardless of who is delivering their model of health care, we have been told: Just trust us, turn your health over to us. We have the answers - follow our advice and you will have a healthier, happier and longer life. This could not be further from the truth. Our health care, or really I should say sickness care systems, are failing and have been failing for some time, even after the general acceptance of preventative, alternative, complementary or integrative medicine. It is very unlikely that socialized, centralized medicine provided by the government and promoted by Michael Moore in *Sicko,* and many liberal politicians will fix the health care dilemma. I believe individuals must take more responsibility for their own health and not depend on others. They must stop overusing the system. Socialized medicine does not transfer the responsibility to the individual and does nothing to curb the overzealous use of doctors and drugs.

Of the most economically advanced free world countries, the US rates near the bottom in health and longevity, and a 178 nation survey of happiness rates the US also near the bottom at 150 out of all the countries surveyed. Figure 1 lists the top twelve causes of death in the United Sates in the year 2001. That list has not changed much in the past several decades with the exception of the increase in death from hospital and doctor related causes and from a rather new disease, Alzheimer's. Both of these categories have increased rapidly. Modern medicine, with the hundreds of billions of dollars spent on research, has not really made much headway in finding the cause of or treating the top diseases.

Top 10 Causes of Death

Heart Disease and Stroke	878,421
Cancer	553,091
Doctor, Drug, and Hospital	125,000 (783,936)
Respiratory	122,009
Accidents	97,900
Diabetes	69,301
Pneumonia	65,313
Alzheimer's	49,558
Kidney diseases	37,251
Infections	31,224

Figure 1

How can this be? In a country that spends more money per capita; has more doctors, nurses, lab technicians per capita; runs more laboratory tests, does more physical therapy, prescribes more drugs and has more hospitals and nursing homes per capita than any other country in the world – why are we not at the top in health and happiness? How can the US produce such dismal statistics? Why in a country where we seem to have the most of everything are we so sick and unhappy?

2.3   Human Genome Project

Great hope was placed on the Human Genome Project but it rendered disappointing results. Humans do not have 125,000 genes as once thought. We only have about 25,000 genes about the same as an earthworm. One gene one protein concept was a fundamental tenet of genetic determination. Eighty percent of the presumed and acquired DNA does not exist. A fruit fly has 15,000 genes – the earthworm has 24,000 genes. David Baltimore, preeminent geneticist and 2001 Nobel Prize winner, says it is clear we humans do not obtain our undoubted complexity over worms and plants by using more genes. Scientists have enucleated cells and the cells can survive up to two months without genes, so the nucleus is not the brain of the cell as previously thought. It is not possible for genetic engineers to fix all our biological dilemmas. There simply are not enough genes to account for the complexity of human life and of human disease. Baltimore states the Human Genome Project forces us to consider other ideas about how life is controlled.

It is time to go back to the beginning and understand how energy and the transcendence of negative to positive energy affect your life.

Some prevention orientated people might say: it is the junk food or the refined food industry's fault; or it is the fault of the big factories and automobiles that are polluting our air and our environment, or it is that we are too lazy and don't walk enough, or the America people are too stressed. While these, as well as other conditions play a role in sickness, in order to better understand why we are so sick in America, we must dispel some beliefs.

2.4   Longevity and Diet

Let's look at diet. Japan, the current leader in longevity may, by some standards, have what some might call a "good diet." Some think the Japanese diet is low in fat and high in fruits and vegetables. Don't be mistaken, they also eat their share of fat and so called junk foods. Japan is not a low stress nation. It is very congested and their workers are driven, work long hours and have considerable external stress. We should not forget that everyone alive in Japan today over 60 years of age endured fall out from the atomic bombs dropped on Hiroshima and Nagasaki at the end of World War II. Why would the people of a country contaminated by radioactive fallout live longer than in other countries that were not contaminated? What is a "good diet?" If the Japanese are thought to eat a good diet and are number one in longevity, how do you account for Austrians, who are number two in longevity and eat an entirely different diet? Austrians eat more fat, protein and sugar than Japanese, yet live nearly as long. Why?

Or how does one account for Chinese who are rated number six in longevity? I don't think a handful of white rice can be considered a good diet and, most who have visited China, agree its big cities are the most polluted on the face of the earth. Congestion is horrible, which makes China a very stressful place to live.

Let's face it; good health and longevity are dependant upon many things. It is multifactorial. There are over 67 different specialties or subspecialties in the sickness care business in the US. None are looking after the total being and how the mind, body and spirit function in the total health process. I contend that the specialty groups have overlooked or misunderstood two major factors that play a big role in the dismal state of the health in America. To better understand health and wellness, it is necessary to look at the basics of many disciplines and philosophies – understanding and incorporating embryology, anatomy and physiology, psychology, and psychiatry. We need to look at ancient Chinese medicine, genetics and developmental anatomy, and then bring them all together, and understand that the mind, body and spirit function as a whole, not as many separate subdivisions.

2.5 Energy Medicine

The only place left to look at the complexity of the human body is energy. Energy medicine will be and is the medicine of the future – here today.

Another missing link of wellness will be covered in a book that I am writing on proprioception and how faulty proprioceptive feedback to the brain affects the autonomic nervous system. This future book will discuss the importance of proprioception from the oral cavity, head and neck area and how faulty signals from this area affect the balance of the sympathetic and parasympathetic branches of the autonomic nervous system. The autonomic nervous system also known to lay people as the automatic or involuntary nervous system controls all of the internal organs including the heart and the stress mechanism. A great deal of medicine is aimed at trying to control symptoms from this area, mostly to no avail. This subject is too lengthy for this short book, but a discussion is available now in my Healing Light DVDs.

Chapter 3

ENERGY BASICS

Be humble for you are made of earth Be noble for you are made of stars.

—*Serbian proverb*

3.1   What is Energy?

What is energy? The physics definition is the capacity of a physical system to do work. The units of energy are measured in joules or ergs, but *energy can take a wide variety of forms. In this book I will be discussing energy as related to universal and human energy.*

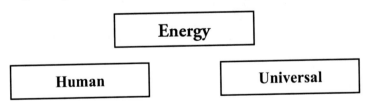

Figure 2

In the beginning GOD created heaven and earth. And God said "let there be light" and there was. And God saw the light and said. That is good. Everything in the Universe is light including our bodies.

Our bodies are just denser so the energy can be seen. Other energy is of a higher vibration and cannot been seen. Auras are examples of higher energy that can only be seen by special photography, such as Kirlian or Bio Liminal photography and by some gifted individuals.

3.2   Sea of Electromagnetic Radiation

Science has demonstrated that we live in a universe we can barely comprehend through our five physical senses. The material universe, the part to which our physical senses have access, is a small portion of the total universe—between two and four percent. The other ninety-six to ninety-eight percent of the universe is energy in the form of electromagnetic radiation. Almost all of this energy is invisible or not detectable to our physical senses. The great English physicist, James Clerk Maxwell, demonstrated the existence of this sea of electromagnetic radiation that, for the first time, expressed the basic laws of electricity and magnetism in a unified fashion. In his electromagnetic theory, published in 1867, Maxwell proved they were two inseparable aspects of one phenomenon—electromagnetic radiation. Maxwell was able to demonstrate that electric and magnetic fields travel through space in the form of waves at the constant speed of light. He first therorized that light is, in fact, undulations in the same medium that is the cause of the electric and magnetic phenomena. Maxwell is considered by many, especially those within the field of physics, to be the scientist of the nineteenth century most influential on twentieth century physics. His contributions to physics are considered by many to be of the same magnitude as those of Newton and Einstein.

Our physical bodies mirror the universe. To our senses, they seem to be solid matter. But when we examine our "solid" matter, we discover the same proportion of matter to energy. Our bodies like all other matter in the universe are composed of atoms. Only two percent of the atom is matter—the center with positively charged protons held together with the neutrally charged neutrons, and the negatively charged electrons circling or orbiting in some pattern around the positively charged proton. Between the center or nucleus of the atom and its electrons is a great deal of space which composes the other ninety-eight percent of the universe. We used to call this space empty. Today we know this space is electromagnetic energy and we have instruments which can detect, map and measure this energy.

Throughout the universe is a uniform electromagnetic field, filling all space that is not matter. This universal electromagnetic field surrounds us and moves within our bodies. It is a measurable phenomenon and a creative principle.

Energy can be as subtle as a thought or as powerful as an atomic bomb. Energy is the essence of life and it cannot be created or destroyed – only converted. An example is burning a log. The form of the log is gone but not the energy. The energy was transformed into heat. It is not any different in our bodies. We eat food and it likewise is transferred into ATP, the energy used by our brain and other organs to carry out body functions.

3.3   Electromagnetic Spectrum

All energy in the universe fits some place on the scale as depicted in the electromagnetic spectrum as shown in figure 3.

ELECTROMAGNETIC SPECTRUM

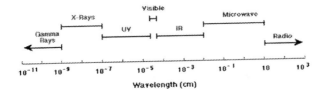

Figure 3

Every electromagnetic wave has two characteristics—it moves horizontally and vibrates vertically. The wavelength is determined by the number of complete cycles that occur in one second, or cycles per second (cps).

These waves are arranged on a continuum according to how rapidly they vibrate. These vibrations are called Hertz, abbreviated Hz. Another way of defining frequency is the number of times the lazy "s" wave is interrupted per second. Regardless of the length of a wave, it can oscillate at different frequencies and these frequencies are very specific. An example that is easy to understand is radio waves. If you tune your radio to 104.1, you may get a country western station. At 104.2, you get static, and at 104.3 you get nothing.

When an organism or an instrument that produces frequency resonates at the optimal frequency and is in harmony with the frequencies that exist around the organism, there is a tendency of the organism to resonate at the frequency established by the stronger of the two oscillations. This explains the "like attracts like" principle and why it is so important to maintain strong positive vibrations to keep and attract more positive vibrations. This also explains why certain people are attracted to other people.

While it is difficult to always be positive, with the development of the low level lasers and the improvement of miniature computers placed inside of the laser instruments, it is easier to accomplish frequency changes and deliver strong signals to the body. This helps overcome the effect of stress, negative thinking and other "downers."[4]

3.4   Wave Length

The type of information any wave carries depends on its length. Wave length is measured in nanometers from peak to peak of the wave. In the visible spectrum, wave length relates to colors. (See figure 4)

WAVELENGTH = COLOR

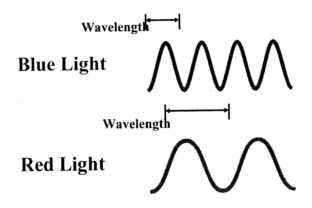

Figure 4

The visible spectrum depicts the colors that we all know so well, the colors of the rainbow and our crayola box. The visible spectrum starts with violet, indigo, green, yellow, orange, red and then into the infrared where the waves are no longer visible. (See figure 5)

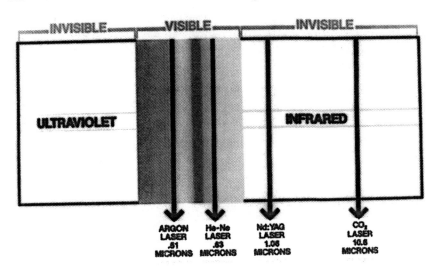

Figure 5

In the visible spectrum blue light is the shorter wave length and red light is the longer wave length. Interference is when two waves are in phase and overlap each other. When two waves are combined, the amplitude of the wave is greater than the amplitude of only a single wave. As amplitude increases, the speed the wave travels also increases and the signal gets stronger, providing more benefits, plus the wave is carried deeper into the tissue. All things on earth have a frequency including cells, tissue and organs. Waves have an infinite capacity to store and transfer information.[5]

Chapter 4

UNIVERSAL ENERGY

We rise to great heights by a winding staircase.
—Francis Bacon

4.1 What is Universal Energy?

Universal energy is composed of four sources.

(1) Electromagnetic field of which the photon is the messenger particle.

(2) Strong force of which the gluons are the smallest bundle.

(3) Weak force with bosons being the smallest particle.

(4) Gravity with the graviton as the smallest particle.

The electromagnetic field is composed of a swarm of photons. Photons are small packets of light energy in the form of a wave element with a defined wavelength and a frequency related to that wavelength.

Two oppositely charged particles interact through the exchange of photons. Photons are not a transmitter of force; rather they are a transfer of information. Photons will attach to and carry electrons.

Electrodynamic fields control all life. These Life Fields become a blueprint for immortality. As light energy travels forward, it also oscillates up and down in a wiggling "lazy letter S" motion called a "sine wave." This energy is before us, in us and around us now and at all times. These up and down oscillations are referred to as "Hertz." It is impossible to adequately diagram all the energy fields interacting with all the other energy fields. But consider an egg beater with all its tines working in harmony swirling its contents around to make something that appears different from what was started. Keep in mind what happens when one of the tines gets bent and the egg beater stops? That is the way it is with energy fields!

Einstein, Planck, Bhor, and modern day physicists Stephen Hawking, Brian Greene and others cannot agree on the energy that makes the universe operate. Quantum mechanics, quantum theory, quantum physics, quantum electrodynamics, general relativity, special relativity, uncertainty principle, quantum chromodynamics, quantum electroweak theory and the string theory, or the theory of everything (TOE) still do not explain our universe, so HOW is it that medicine can be so certain about the germ theory and what causes disease?[6] The Sun is our greatest source of energy. It not only gives heat but also light. The sunlight can burn and it can also heal. Without sunlight your body would be unable to make Vitamin D. Light is pure energy and, according to Einstein's formula $E=mc^2$; where E = energy, m = mass, c = speed of light. Light is an integral component of the energy equation; however Einstein's formula still does not explain non-local energy which is everywhere at once. Einstein never said his work was facts, only theory.

4.2 An Alternative Model

As a result of this view of the universe, the world is becoming a soulless place. Life has lost much of its meaning. People are suffering from the effects of living lives based on alienation, loneliness, stress, disease, anxiety and fear. The ills of society are so deeply rooted they seem impossible to cure. To accept these ills in order to live a life of convenience is to surrender any possibility of meaning, and to rule out the achievement of total abundance.

There is a more rewarding model, one that can lead to unity and wholeness, one that will bring meaning to your life. Obviously, you are more than your physical body. The material parts of your body are constantly changing. Yet you remain the same person. The creative energy field that holds you together in a recognizable form is your essence. Your essence is unchanging. It is the same energy that fills the universe, but it has individualized to form you.

The Universal Mind operates according to certain laws. As Albert Einstein said, "The most incomprehensible thing about the universe is its comprehensibility." We can indeed understand how our universe works. Our science has discovered certain laws that predict the way matter is created and the way energy interacts with matter. These laws also apply to the interactions between the Universal Mind and our physical selves. It is by understanding and working with these laws that we become complete and discover our purpose in life.

4.3   The Laws of Thermodynamics

There are two laws of thermodynamics. These two laws give us incredible insight into what life is. They contain the overall picture of the meaning of your temporal life on earth and your eternal life in the universe.

The first law of thermodynamics states that energy can never be created or destroyed. Energy is conserved. The total amount of energy remains constant.

Since each of us is a unique individual physical body, each of us had to have been created by a unique energy field. The unique energy field that created, and is us, could not have been made since energy cannot be created. The only way our unique creative energy field could have come into existence was by separating from the universal creative energy that fills the universe and us. A very tiny portion of universal creative energy was transformed into the unique energy field that produced your physical body. That unique energy field is you and you alone. It is your essence.

Your essence is pure energy. Therefore it does not age, and cannot be destroyed. It remains a permanent part of the universe. When you were created, you were created as an individual - unique only to your electromagnetic field. You are immortal. You have a unique energy field that is eternal. You are an eternal self.

The second law of thermodynamics states that any closed system that uses energy always goes from a more organized to a less organized form. Whenever energy is used to perform any work, most of it is used in performing the work, but some of it is always lost into the atmosphere and cannot be recovered. Thus whenever we do any work, or take any action, some energy is irretrievably lost. There is less energy available after the work is completed than there was at the beginning.

A common example is the light bulb. Electrical energy is used to heat the filament until it glows and radiates light. However, some of the energy turns into heat and is lost into the environment. You know this is true by touching a light bulb that has been burning for any length of time and feel the heat. Eventually, due to the loss of energy, the bulb burns out.

According to the second law, closed systems that do work—and we all are closed systems that do work—move from order to disorder. In time any closed system will become a disordered system. The word the scientists use to describe this increase of disorder is "entropy." In all closed systems over a period of time entropy increases. Disorder always increases; it never decreases. Every appliance or automobile reaches such a state of disorder that it ceases to function. Every oak tree dies.

Your physical body is a closed system; therefore every day it becomes more of a disordered system. When disorder reaches the level at which your physical body ceases to function, we call it death and imply an ending but, in fact, the physical body is doing nothing more than following the second law of thermodynamics.

The first law states that energy cannot be created or destroyed and is eternal. However, all the matter in the universe, including our physical selves, experiences entropy and is, consequently, temporary. Thus, our temporal body must stop functioning. Our eternal self, since it is energy, continues. Our eternal self cannot be destroyed because it is pure energy.

Why does the Universal Mind separate unique energy fields from itself and create temporal beings?

Universal creative energy is totally impersonal. It fills the universe and is the same everywhere. However, change and evolution are constant activities of energy. Universal energy evolves by separating from itself packages of individualized creative energy. It creates components that have the capacity to evolve to higher levels. The Universal Mind creates us in order to evolve itself to higher levels.

4.4   Who, What and Why Are We?

Who are we? Where did we come from? Why are we here? There is nothing more important in your life than your answers to these questions. Your answers will flow through every meditation in this book, and most importantly, through every part of your life.

The research of physics and the two laws of thermodynamics have shown us that the material world is created by energy. Einstein's famous formula E=MC squared expresses this fact.

Therefore, since each of our human bodies is material, each of us is created by an energy source. Since every human being is different from every other human being, every one of us has been created by an energy source that is unique to each of us.

Most of us have been taught to believe that we are our physical body. But our physical body is always changing. All of the protein in your body is continually being replaced. Energy goes around and comes around. You are eternal.

Every seven years every single atom in your body and every single part of you dies and is replaced. But you are still you. Look at photographs of yourself at ages ten, twenty, thirty and etc. Each photograph is very different from the preceding one, but they are all you. If you are your body, which picture are you, because they are all very different? Think of it—over the course of seven years your body completely dies, yet you live on! Obviously you are more than just your body.

You were not created only at conception; you are continually being created every second. If you were only your physical body, your life would be extremely short. You are both your physical body and the energy source that created it. As explained by the two laws of thermodynamics, your body—which is material—is temporary and is always physically deteriorating. However, your energy source is permanent. It can never be destroyed, it can only be transformed.

How then did the energy source that is you come into existence? Energy cannot be created. Energy creates matter, not more energy. Therefore, where did your energy source come from?

The only way it could have come into existence was to have separated from the universal creative energy, the universal energy that is our creator. Our western world calls it God; it has many other names. In order for each of us to be, our creator separated from itself tiny energy sources designed for the creation of each of us. Each of us is a separation from our creator, yet each of us is a little bit of our creator!

4.5 Why then was our physical body created? Why are we here?

Our creator already is and has everything. Our creator cannot evolve to anything more. However, the universal law of evolution tells us that the universe "He" created is always changing and evolving into more, into higher levels of being. The only way our universe and its creator can become more is by having parts of it become more. You are a part of the universe. Therefore, whenever you become more, whenever you evolve into more, the entire universe evolves into more. The mission of each of us on earth is to use our temporary human life to evolve to our highest possible level, and by so doing evolve the entire universe to a higher level.

You can do this because your life on earth is a co-creational experience. Your energy source originally created you. Since your energy source is energy and therefore eternal, you call it your eternal self, or your essence. Now, during your life on earth, your mission is to evolve your eternal self to the highest level possible. How do you do that? Each time you evolve your human self to a higher level, you also evolve your eternal self to a higher level.

Your earth life is your means for achieving a richer existence for your eternal self and your eternal life. However, you will find that in so doing you will also achieve the richest possible life for yourself on earth. A life of evolution for your eternal self is a life of bliss for your trip on earth.

The meditations you are about to learn will be your step-by-step guide to wealth and joy on earth. But they are not your end goal. They are the means to achieving the highest possible evolution of your eternal self to greater and greater levels of being. When your "life" on earth ceases, your eternal self will be far more evolved than when it began. That is the purpose and mission of your life on earth. When your life on earth ends, your eternal self is ready to move ahead full speed into a much more exciting next step in your eternal journey.

4.6 Newton's Laws of Motion

Energy is always in motion. The laws governing this motion were first described by Sir Isaac Newton. Newton's first law of motion says, "Every body continues in its state of rest, or of uniform motion in a straight line, unless it is compelled to change that state by forces impressed on it."

Applying this law of motion to our lives on this earth, we can know that everything that happens to us is the result of the specific actions we take. Our actions are the equivalent of Newton's forces. Far more effective than trying to correct a specific problem we're having, is to change our actions that are causing the problem. Through this book, we will learn which of our actions are appropriate for us and conducive to abundance, and which are inappropriate and getting in the way of abundance.

Newton's second law states, "Force equals mass times acceleration." This is the law that lets us know of our capacity for controlling the quality of the forces being applied to our lives. Since mass and acceleration are easily changed, then the force that is their result is mutable as well. This means that once you understand the forces affecting your life, you have the power to change them. The process of applied active meditation you are about to learn will enable you to take control of the forces influencing all areas of your life.

Newton's third law states, "For every action, there is an equal and opposite reaction." This tells us we live in a bipolar universe that the forces affecting us come in opposite pairs. That is to say, every force in our life immediately produces another force that is opposite to it. This is one of the most important laws for you to apply to your daily life. Because of it, you can be sure whenever you experience something that produces negative or harmful effects in your life, there is available an opposing something that will produce positive and healthy effects.

The universe is neither good nor bad. It is both good and bad simultaneously. A major aim of the program of applied active meditation is the development of your ability to tune into the positive force that goes along with any negative one you may be experiencing. When you use meditation you deactivate the negative force and bring its positive opposite into play.

4.7   Movement toward Evolution and Harmony

By putting the laws of thermodynamics and those of motion together, we know the universe is in a constant state of motion and change. This change wants to be in the direction of evolution, of becoming more. You cannot stop this constant change, but you can influence it. You are in charge of the amount and direction of the change that takes place through you. If you direct your changes toward growth and evolution, you will be moving in accord with the universe. If you resist evolution, you will be at odds with the universe.

Every change in the universe also aims at achieving harmony. When your actions increase harmony in the universe, you are contributing toward universal harmony. When your actions disrupt harmony, you are disrupting universal harmony.

Your job in this life is to obey the universal laws and move your life in the direction of evolution and harmony. Your eternal self is a package of individualized creative energy that has the potential for growth. Because through you it has taken on physical form, your eternal self now can communicate with both the material world and the Universal Mind. By combining your daily material experiences with the Universal Mind, you can accomplish the job for which you were created. In the process, you will achieve the highest abundance possible on earth! When the time comes for your body to cease functioning, you take nothing material with you. You will, however, take all the Universal Mind you have accumulated.

4.8   Black Hole and Zero Point Field

The black hole or zero point field gives current physicists a model to help understand the Universal Mind.

Physicists refer to the black hole as a "vacuum" or the zero point field, because fluctuations in the field are still detectable at temperatures of absolute zero. It is the lowest possible energy in the emptiest state of space where all energy and matter has been removed.

What is in this field that has no volume or mass? A surplus or deficit of electrons creates an electrical charge which is surrounded by an electric and magnetic field. What is between the positive and negative charge of the atom? Why do stable-looking atoms, without apparent cause lose electrons, and where do these electrons go? In the subatomic world, the ability of an electron to influence another quantum particle instantaneously over any distance without any measurable force or energy is termed "nonlocality." This sort of emission and re-absorption not only occurs among photons and electrons, but all quantum particles in the universe. While quantum scientists do not know why an electron orbits around a proton, it is known that the entire universe is a "sea of light," moving in a constant sideways or lazy "s" curve and always in constant motion. Most of this sea of light is in wavelengths the eye cannot detect.

Zero point field changes the theory of quantum mechanics. In the zero point field the energy level of any known particle can not be pinpointed because it is always changing. However, all subatomic particles possess a tiny residual movement and always radiate some type yet to be named energy. Thus this empty space is bursting with activity. The zero point field is a repository of all fields and all ground energy states and all virtual particles. It is a field of all fields.

4.9   Primary Perception

Another example of subtle universal energy is primary perception and how subtle energy relates to plant communication. You undoubtedly know someone with a "green thumb." Their plants just seem to do well. Did you ever stop to think it might be the person's subtle energy resonating with the plants - not unlike the *Horse Whisper*, where human frequencies resonate with horses, or the *Dog Whisper*, where they resonate with dogs? To study how plants communicate, I recommend Cleve Backster's book *Primary Perception*. Backster was a leading expert in lie detection and worked for the FBI and many police departments around the US, teaching others to interpret lie detector tests. During one testing, he noticed that a plant next to the person he was testing wilted when ever the subject lied. This led Backster to adapt similar devices to plants and has shown how plants communicate. When I visited his lab in San Diego, we applied the frequency of mode 1 of the Q Laser System (See Chapter 12) to a sickly plant and it immediately registered on Cleve's detection device as a positive energy. The plant liked it and its wilted leaves perked up right before our eyes. *Primary Perception* is hailed worldwide as a major subtle energy breakthrough on plants. Backster's books are available in most major book stores and in several languages.

Chapter 5

CREATIVE ENERGY

If the doors of perception were cleansed everything would appear as it is, infinite
-- William Blake, "A Memorable Fancy"

5.1   Blueprint for Immortality

Dr. Harold Saxton Burr, who taught neuroanatomy at the Yale University School of Medicine for nearly fifty years, investigated what he called the "electric patterns of life." In 1972, he published a breakthrough work called *Blueprint for Immortality.*

Burr discovered that all material forms, including human bodies, are ordered and controlled by "electro-dynamic fields which can be measured and mapped with precision." Inherent in these fields, he said, is the power to direct the growth and development of any living system.

Burr called the electro-dynamic fields that he measured "L Fields," meaning life fields. "Until modern instruments revealed the existence of the controlling L Fields," he wrote, "biologists were at a loss to explain how our bodies 'keep in shape' through ceaseless metabolism and changes of material."

Modern research with "tagged" elements, demonstrates the material of our bodies is constantly in flux. For example, all the protein in your body is turned over every six months. If I do not see you for six months, when we meet again, I will not see one molecule that was there six months earlier. Yet the new molecules are put together in such a way that they form exactly you and you alone, and I easily recognize you.

The electromagnetic field is composed of a swarm of photons. Two oppositely charged particles interact through the exchange of photons. Photons are not a transmitter of force; rather they are a transfer of information. Photons will attach to and carry electrons.

The greatest discovery in science was the verification that all matter is composed of atoms, first proposed in 1803 by English chemist John Dalton. All disciplines of science are derived from that fact. The second greatest theory came in 1905 when Einstein published general relativity, showing that the presence of mass and energy "curves" space-time and this curvature affects the path of free particles and even the path of light. There are some physicists that think the third greatest theory, may be the Aether Physics Model, which believes that all particles and fields have their basis in a dynamic, quantum-scale, called the Aether.

5.2   Where Do Photons Come From?

In the beginning, God said "let there be light. He saw the light and said that is good." But what is light?

A scientific expalantion was first presented in the late 19th century with the luminiferous Aether theory. Aether was the term used to describe a medium for the propagation of light. When Einstein developed his therory of special relativity he formulated it without the Aether concept, and today the Aether is considered to be a superseded scientific concept. Certainly today most physicists believe there must be an explanation beyond Einstein's special realativity for the substance that fills the upper regions of space, beyond the clouds. Dark matter is a term used today. Whether this life controlling energy comes from God, the Aether or dark matter, it is all the same – it was created by a greater force – it is up to us to learn to use it for the good of ourselves and humankind.

5.3   What is the Casimir Effect – Aether?

The Casimir effect is a small attractive force which acts between two close parallel *uncharged* conducting plates. It is due to quantum vacuum fluctuations of the electromagnetic field. The effect was predicted by the Dutch physicist, Hendrick Casimir, in 1948. According to the quantum theory, the vacuum contains virtual particles which are in a continuous state of fluctuation. The energy density decreases as the plates are moved closer, which implies there is a small force drawing them together. This force has been defined as, "a force from nothing."

Some cultures call this energy "Life Force" or chi or prana. Others call it Aether derived energy or Salutogenesis. Salutogenesis is the organism's way of healing itself with energy. Dr. Albert Szent Gyorgyi, world renowned physician and the 1937 Nobel Prize winner for his discovery of vitamin C said: "In every culture and in every medical tradition before ours, healing was accomplished by moving energy." The body is an electro-chemical unit. For generations scientists have studied the chemical aspect of the body, now is the time to concentrate on the electrical - the energy part.

While Aether is not energy in and of itself, it is converted to energy via creation of the photon via the Casmir effect. Aether derived energy can be transferred by laying on of hands, prayer, sexual intercourse, positive thinking, being in a positive atmosphere, and by subtle energy low level lasers. To be effective these lasers must resonate with the body's energy and deliver lost electrons via photons to damaged cells throughout the body. (See Chapter 12)

When some cells or a part of you dies, there still will be some part of you that will not die. That something replaces your dead atoms and molecules and puts new ones together into exactly you and you alone. That something is the creative energy field that forms you into a unique being. As Burr put it, "The electro-dynamic field of the body serves as a matrix or mold, which preserves the arrangement and activities and functions of the body."

After years of mapping and measuring L Fields, Burr declared that the essence of a human being is pure energy. His conclusions have been verified and amplified by the work of Dr. Fritz-Albert Popp, a German physicist, who has, in Munich, the largest biophoton laboratory in the world. Using a photon multiplier as his chief measuring instrument, Popp has shown that every cell in the human body communicates with every other cell by means of electromagnetic radiation. Popp's research provides further evidence that the physiological functions of living organisms are controlled and regulated by electromagnetic field patterns.

Photons are packages of energy. Biophotons are packages of energy transmitted by living organisms. Popp found that biophotons are electromagnetic waves with high frequencies. He also discovered that in the human body DNA has the role of absorbing and transmitting biophotons. Thus DNA controls the biochemical and physiological reactions of every cell.

DNA does this by sending out "written" instructions in the form of RNA. When the electromagnetic field is working right with a balance of energy, the DNA keeps the body functioning correctly through its RNA messages. When the electromagnetic field is interfered with, DNA sends out faulty messages, and the body functions incorrectly. Thus, at a basic level, the cause of any disease is incorrect information resulting from a flawed electromagnetic field pattern. When cancer cells grow wild and destroy instead of cooperating, they have, as Popp puts it, "lost the possibility of taking up mutual photons from each other."

Chapter 6

HUMAN ENERGY

A pupil from whom nothing is ever demanded which he cannot do,
never does all he can.

–John Stuart Mill

6.1 Homeostasis

The state of one's energy manifests health or illness. Managing one's energy determines homeostasis. Homeostasis is maintained by ongoing information transfer between frequencies of consciousness, energy and matter. I will repeat the word homeostasis often. We know what the word means but few ever find the formula to maintain homeostasis in all muscle, glandular, organ and energy systems. Not to include all aspects of nature, i.e. physiology, electromagnetic energy, subtle energy, and consciousness, is to ignore data and limit understanding of homeostasis.[8]

As stated, our bodies are electro-chemical units. For generations scientists have studied the chemical aspect of the body, now it is time to concentrate on the electrical part. Scientists cannot provide an avenue to physical and mental health by <u>studying sickness and disease any more than they can create sanity by studying madness.</u>

Medicine is being forced to accept that energy not only plays a role in illness; it also plays a major role in staying well and certainly in the quality of life. When the body is in homeostasis there is no illness. The body should be maintained by ongoing information transfer between frequencies of consciousness, energy and matter. Our bodies are just energy. When you die, if you choose to be cremated, 99% of your body mass goes up as energy in the form of heat. The remaining 1% is still energy in the form of charged minerals. The energy of the body is perpetual.

Our bodies make their own photons called biophotons which are small packets of coherent infrared light generated and emitted by our own cells for intercellular communication. Coherence means the photons are well-ordered or are in synchronicity. This is the major difference of how light works either in or out of the body. Coherence is the difference between regular light, such as incandescent light, LEDs on the dash of your car and true lasers. Regular light and LEDs cannot carry information – they cannot check out your groceries, copy your print or play your music. Only low level lasers can do all of these things. Lasers of different wavelengths have different energy levels and subsequently provide different results to different cells of the body.

A person with strong vitality and lack of inner stress emits more photons. With balanced universal energy fields, these biophotons combine to form soliton waves – that is, the biophotons now have increased velocity producing an aura which is able to be imaged via Kirlian photography or newer imaging techniques, such as bio-liminal photography.

Some gifted people like Jack Schwarz can elevate their frequency to levels that allow them to read auras. Since healthy cells and organs are charged and emit energy in the form of light and sick cells and organs do not emit energy, then these gifted people, by reading breaks in the aura, can even diagnose which organs might be malfunctioning. Cellular biophoton emission and biophoton intercellular communication is altered by many things such as medication, life style, quality of food, food sensitivities, environment, emotional conflicts and stability. These and other factors affect your vitality.

6.2 The Jack Schwarz Story

As you read in the preface, Jack Schwarz was a remarkable young man. He was an 18 year old Hollander who during World War II was captured and imprisoned in one of the Holocaust camps. This 200 lb young man was starved down to 90 lbs. He was beaten, his skin cut and his bones were broken. He was dehydrated and each day after the beatings was dragged back to his cell to die. He soon realized that if he concentrated on his pain, his problems, his situation, it was unbearable. He knew he would die like most other Holocaust prisoners unless he did something different. What he did to take his mind off his beatings, his cut, broken and bruised body was to focus on a fly or a spec on the wall. He practiced zooming the smooth muscles of the eyes so the fly would appear as a big bird in front of his face, then he would push it out to infinity so it was just a small spec. When he was doing this non-mental, spiritual exercise, he had no pain. To Schwarz's amazement, when he came out of what you might call a "trance," his body was healed. His cuts and broken bones were healed without any nutrition, vitamins, minerals or enzymes. How did he do that? This contradicts everything that has been taught in medicine and nutrition today.

Schwarz eventually escaped from the holocaust camp and came to America. After demonstrating his unexplained healing skills to laypeople in Portland, Oregon, he was encouraged to go to the Menninger Institute in Topeka, Kansas, for them to study how he accomplished these spectacular feats. Menninger is one of the premier brain research centers in the US. While studying Schwarz and yogis at Menninger, it was learned they healed themselves by controlling their energy. They did this not by concentrating on the injury but by just learning to "let go" and transcend the negative to the positive. They were attracting electrons from the universe and were transferring them to the injured cells. They were able to put themselves in brain waves that allowed instant pain control and healing. More than once Schwarz demonstrated pushing a large needle through his arm and controlling the bleeding and healing the wound before the eyes of researchers and medical doctors. This sounds impossible, but as one of my teachers said "if it happened, it must be possible." The universal waves that Schwarz unknowingly produced appeared to be miracle healing. These waves came from his subconscious control over his conscious mind by accessing universal energy. He was able to turn off his conscious mind; otherwise this could not have been done. Frequencies can be constructive or destructive and some individuals have transcended those frequencies without any outside assistance. When I studied with Jack Schwarz, I questioned what appeared to me to be miracles and wrote them off as something extremely unusual and thought they belonged in a carnival side show, not in medicine or science. When I said to Jack: "you are different;" he replied: "no Larry, I am not different, I have just learned to unlock it and you have not – all people have the same ability." I kept thinking about what he was unlocking. What was he doing that was different? How did I miss this in my medical/dental training? I kept repeating to myself – if it happened it must be true. It was at this time in my life that I set out to find out how to unlock the special frequencies in myself and in others and to make a difference in humankind. The Jack Schwartz method eventually worked for me but it took a long time to learn. I kept asking myself; was there a better way to learn to access frequencies from the universe like Schwarz did? The outcome of those efforts culminated in the development of Q Laser System which produces frequencies like Schwarz used to heal himself.

6.3   This is Not a Miracle

To some, it might appear that what Jack Schwarz, Bill Tiller, Yogis and ancient Tibetan holy men accomplished is nothing short of miraculous. If you only believe in the conscious and subconscious mind, then it might seem like miracles, but if you transcend to the Universal Mind and combine that with the very basics of science from the conscious mind, accepting that it is not a miracle becomes easier. You, like the great healers, have the same ability. Understanding the basics will help you unlock that ability.

6.4   Atoms

Our physical bodies mirror the universe. To our senses, they seem to be solid matter. However, when we examine our "solid" matter, we discover the same proportion of matter to energy. Our bodies like all other matter in the universe are composed of atoms. Everything on Earth is supposedly composed of atoms, including the human body. Deepak Chopra, the famed Indian physician, says humans are just electrical energy with a lot of empty space between the positive and negative charges. Scientists still do not know why electrons orbit around protons and then for unknown reasons, these elusive negative charges move away from the positive charged proton. However they do know that when charges oscillate at lower frequencies the object becomes denser and is visible to the eye. You have heard the saying: "he really is dense" which usually means the person isn't very smart or his head is dense – thus the saying; "he is hard headed." All humans are dense and vibrate at lower frequencies which make us visible. We come back to trying to understand what is in the empty space between the positive and negative charges and how it affects humankind. Figure 6 depicts the atom from the Newtonian theory of science where the nucleus and electrons of the atom can be diagramed and presumably have mass.

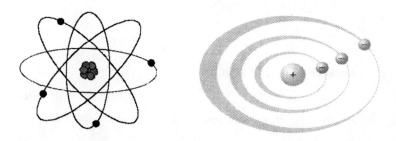

Figure 6

The modern energy theory is that atoms in and of themselves cannot be diagrammed as seen in figure 6 and are better explained as just energy as in figure 7. The atom is just energy – no mass – just nothing unless combined, then we have something. Only two percent of the atom is matter—the center with positively charged protons and neutrons and the negatively charged electrons circling the center. Between the center or nucleus of the atom and its electrons is a great deal of space that accounts for the other ninety-eight percent. We used to call this empty. Today we know this space is teeming with electromagnetic energy. Universal energy is everywhere and is dependent upon the observer. I encourage you to watch the movie *What the Bleep Do We Know*, or the newer longer version *How Far Down the Rabbit Hole Do You Want to Go*. Another new movie that sheds light on universal energy is, *The Secret*.

Figure 7

When twenty of these seemingly massless atoms are combined we have calcium, an element with mass with an atomic weight of 40.078 and a density of 1.55 g/cc. (See figure 8)

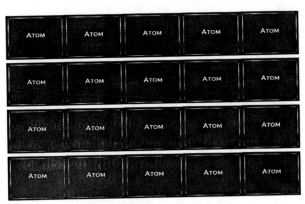

Twenty atoms = Calcium

Figure 8

Science has demonstrated that we live in a universe we can barely comprehend through our five physical senses. The material universe, the part to which our physical senses have access, is a small portion of the total universe—between two and four percent. The other ninety-six to ninety-eight percent is energy in the form of electromagnetic radiation. Almost all of this energy is invisible to our physical senses as explained in chapter 2.

Throughout the universe is a uniform electromagnetic field, filling all space that is not matter. This universal electromagnetic field surrounds us and moves within our bodies. It is a measurable phenomenon and a creative principle. IT IS US.

6.5 Cells

A good in depth book on cells is the *Wisdom of Your Cells* by Dr. Bruce Lipton. This short overview will introduce you to some basics.

There are trillions of forever changing cells in your body. You also have tens of trillions of microbial cells that are energy and respond to other frequencies of energy. Cells are composed of atoms, and as stated, atoms are composed of a very stable positive charged nucleus, the proton, with very unstable negatively charged electrons orbiting in varying elliptical patterns around the nucleus. This fact makes the cells quite unstable.

An atom that gains or loses an electron and becomes either positively or negatively charged is an ion. A hydrogen ion is a hydrogen atom (single proton) that loses its electron and is positively charged. An atom cannot gain or lose a proton. Another way of saying this is: a hydrogen ion is a proton thus a hydrogen ion and a proton are the same thing. Since cells are composed of atoms, we must be very concerned why the atom, and subsequently the cell, loses electrons.

6.6   Ph – Potential Hydrogen

Ph stands for "potential hydrogen." Many nutritionally conscious people are concerned about being to acidic and try to eat an alkalizing diet – failing to realize that Ph is determined by the amount of hydrogen ions present – that is a hydrogen atom that has lost its electron. More hydrogen ions means the body is more acid and fewer hydrogen ions mean it is more alkaline. Hydrogen ions determine if your body fluids are acid or alkaline. Then whether your body is acid or alkaline depends on an electrical charge and not necessarily nutrition. Lower Ph indicates an excess of hydrogen ions so the more acid an organ, then the greater the number of hydrogen ions present and the greater the positive electrical charge. Functional Ph is the Ph that produces a balanced bioenergy and functional health in specific body parts or organs. It is measured on a scale from 0 -14 with 7 being neutral. Acid is 0 – 7 and alkalinity is 7 – 14. Different organ systems have different Ph. The functional Ph of the saliva is 6.4 to 6.8. The functional Ph of the stomach is 1.2 to 2.0. The functional Ph of the intestine is 8.0. When the functional Ph or hydrogen ion concentration of an organ is out of balance, the organ will be weak. It loses electrons faster and becomes "sick". You will learn in chapter 12 that resonating low level lasers puts the electrons back, balances the Ph and strengthens the organ.

6.7   Piezoelectric

Your cells talk to one another by light and with electrical energy called *piezoelectric*. All of the body's cells simultaneously respond at every level and simultaneously signal the entire system. The cells are arranged in a crystalline manner and generate an electrical field when compressed or stretched. This principle is one reason why massage is valuable. The piezoelectric principle supports the biophoton principle, explained later, which tells us how cells communicate instantly through out the body via light and electricity. The Chinese explained this energy flow as chi in the chakra and meridian system. The new break though is that these delicate systems can be altered by resonating low level lasers which put electrons back to the cell membrane[9]

6.8   Redox

Are you taking antioxidants? If you are, you are hoping that the vitamin A and C, zinc, selenium and other nutritional substances, will help control oxidation – the rusting out effect of the body. A simplified explanation of oxidation is explained in what nutritionists call the Redox potential. It describes the quality of a system measured in millivolts either as electron rich referred to as reduced or electron poor referred to as oxidized. This reduced or oxidized principle is based upon presence or absence of electrons at the cell level which in turn regulate organ function. Changes in oxidation affect activation of your genes, the transport of proteins; and influence the production of cytokines which are involved in your immune system. So, you see, again, it is the loss of electrons that controls oxidation as well as cell communication. When you master energy transcendence you can take electrons from the universe and use them as needed at the cell level. Until you master this you can use low level lasers as an antioxidant.

6.9   Nitric Oxide

Nitric oxide is a rather new term to most doctors as well as lay people. Nitric oxide is not the same as Nitrous Oxide or laughing gas used in dental offices. Nitric oxide abbreviated NO is a cellular signaling chemical used throughout the body to carry on cell to cell communication. It is a tiny gaseous, electrically neutral, highly reactive and short lived molecule that is supposed to be made by your own cells. It easily diffuses through cell membranes and carries valuable information from cell to cell. NO serves as bioregulators of your antioxidant (redox metabolism) level and also regulates your immunity. When your cells do not make enough NO, your health begins to deteriorate and you will get sick. Nitric oxide is low in people with cancer and autoimmune diseases. Certain nutrition and resonating low level lasers increase your own cells production of these important messengers. A great deal of cellular health and metabolism is due to the electrical charge of the cell membrane or the loss of electrons. Again we see that the photon emitting low level lasers delivers electrons back to the cell and increases the body's production of NO.[10]

6.10 New information on cellular communication

Further evidence of the role low level lasers play in this important cellular communication is supported by IONS research department in March – May 2006 issue of *Shifts*. It reports a University of Milan study on neuron cell cultures. One sample of neuron cultures was shielded from laser stimulation by being placed under a Faraday copper cage which is used in research to block out electromagnetic forces. The other cultures not under the Faraday cage were stimulated with low level laser radiation and both cultures responded as if they had been stimulated. This is evidence that laser energy controls cellular homeostasis and is not controlled by the electromagnetic forces.

When cells lose electrons and the DNA is altered, the new cells produced are not as healthy as the original cells prior to the loss of electrons. This results in disease, sickness, and aging. In chapter 12 you will learn more how low level laser energy;

1. Restores the lost electrons

2. Normalizes DNA

3. Enhances cellular redox (antioxidant) activity

4. Balances the sodium/potassium pump thus helps in eliminating fluid retention and weight gain and

5. Produces endorphins to control pain and makes the cell healthier overall.

According to Dr. Popp, the universal electromagnetic field is the base for cell communication. It is the most fundamental base of communication, because it works between all cells, between all the single systems of cells and between all molecules with the highest speed which is possible - the speed of light.

Cell to cell communication is necessary for proper tissue, organ and body function. But how do cells communicate? There has been much research in this area and new evidence is surfacing based upon this new wave of energy medicine.

A review of the scientific research shows that cells respond and re-organize as a result of the electromagnetic fields that are directly introduced into that cell

Frequencies at varying rates not only have the ability to alter, the cells but also can alter energy fields, chakras and organ systems. The human body is composed of liquid crystalline and crystalline lattice type molecules. Sine waves travel to the energy field and physical body producing a resonance or vibration of the crystalline structure.[10]

Electromagnetic fields introduced into the cell at varying frequencies alter specific cells, energy fields, charkas, and organ systems of the body. The body simultaneously responds at every level and each part simultaneously signals the entire system creating a super communication system. This kinetic effect causes a rippling effect in the living cellular matrix and sends a piezoelectric signal to all parts of the body.[11]

6.11 Biophotons

Your cells, tissue and organs communicate by producing their own light called biophotons. This infrared light is produced by many different frequencies and with many soliton waves.

Your mind via the Universal Mind has the ability to deliver frequencies as do low level lasers. Optimal frequencies that are in harmony with the frequencies that exist around the organism strengthen the subtle energy fields. If the frequency of an organ, like the pancreas, is known and either with your mind or with sophisticated computer controlled low level lasers, that frequency is exactly reproduced and delivered back to the pancreas, it will heal. To accomplish this without a laser, you raise your excitement level so the energy will reach your pancreas. Low level lasers must be properly programmed in order to deliver electrons back to the sick or injured pancreas. This process is referred to as constructive interference. (See figure 9) Intent and fear exhibited by the user or technician, doctor, and family are major factors in information transfer and can interfere with the subtle energy of constructive interference.

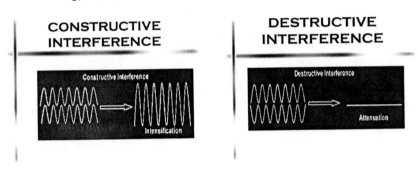

CONSTRUCTIVE INTERFERENCE	DESTRUCTIVE INTERFERENCE

Figure 9   Figure 10

Destructive interference occurs when the waves are out of phase, that is, one wave is peaking as the other is troughing. Destructive interference waves like constructive interference waves have increased amplitude and are able to penetrate deeper into the body without losing their benefits. If the frequency of a bacteria, virus, or fungus is known and is generated by your contact with the Universal Mind or by low level lasers, the destructive frequency can be cancelled and rendered harmless or inactive. Destructive frequency generation and cancellation is a much safer and precise way of controlling harmful bacterial and virus than chemicals and antibiotics which can destroy the flora balance in the body. Destructive frequency cancellation is much like turning off your radio and canceling the radio waves. Generating constructive or destructive interference frequencies are dependent upon a precise computer controlled low level lasers. (See figure 9 and 10)

Chapter 7

BRAIN

I use not only the brains I have, but all I can borrow
— Woodrow Wilson

7.1 Five Brain Waves

The brain consists of the collective activity of hundreds of thousands of neurons functioning by sending brain waves called Hertz over the network. Brain waves can be recorded on an instrument called an electroencephalogram or EEG. Brain waves were first recorded in the late 1800s, about the same time electrocardiogram or EKG for the heart was discovered.

There are five different brain waves, delta, theta, alpha, beta, and gamma, measured in cycles per second called Hertz. Different ranges of Hertz are recorded with a different name and there may be some overlap depending on who you study. There are some differences where one group starts and other stops but if there is no brain wave, you are brain dead.

7.2 Delta Brain Waves

Delta brain waves are from .5 to 4 Hz. These are slow long brain waves as recorded in the near death experience, coma, deep mediation or deep sleep. Those that have witnessed the near death experience report a tunnel of white swirling light – a very peaceful place. Some people report hearing or seeing their God. Various cultures have their individual methods of getting into Delta brain waves. Native Americans practice the Sun Dance where they fast and chant. They do not eat or drink anything for five days while tethered to a tree with leather or rope throngs pierced through the skin on their chest or back. They stay in this position, chanting from the rising of the morning star to sunset, day after day, until they hallucinate and become one with the universe. Yogis do a similar thing, by sitting on a mountain top, in a state of deep meditation, also abstaining from food or water. Shamans also fast, then go to the top of a mountain where they are struck by lightening – the ultimate test of becoming one with the universe. Delta brain waves can be very debilitating or they can heal. Unless you have experienced one of the above situations, you most likely will not be able to benefit from the immediate healing of the Delta brain waves.

Deepak Chopra reported a case history of a young man who was working on a metal roof. He reached down to move a high powered transmission line, which was supposed to have been disconnected. It was not and he was electrocuted and his heart stopped. The electricity went through his hand, through his body and blew his leg into shreds as it exited. It blew him off the two story roof, and when he landed, he landed on his chest and re-started his heart. His co-workers placed him in the back of a station wagon and rushed him to the hospital. On the way to the hospital he experienced the near death phenomenon. This happens when the brain waves are below .5 Hz for a short time. For the victim it seems an eternity and they witness the white swirling tunnel type light. It is reported as being very peaceful.

This young man drifted in and out of these very low Delta brain waves fading in and out of consciousness. When conscious, the doctors repeatedly asked him to sign a release so they could operate and remove his mangled leg. He refused and immediately put himself back in the low Delta brain waves. This is what doctors call a coma – only in this mans case he had learned to control the brain waves. Three weeks later he walked out of the hospital on a completely healed leg. Was this a miracle or had he, like Jack Schwarz, learned to unlock the instant healing brain waves?

Dr. Herbert Benson, author of the *Relaxation Response* reports a similar energy healing with the re-growth of six inches of new bone in the leg of a trapper who got gangrene in his leg after being caught in a bear trap. You also have the opportunity to learn to go there and harness these brain frequencies, if you learn the secret. It starts with letting go of your belief that it is impossible and then practice the methods outlined in *Energy Transcendence*.

7.3   Theta Brain Waves

Theta brain waves are from 4 to approximately 8 Hz. Theta brain waves occur when you are asleep. While sleep gives the body and its organs a chance to rest and revive, there is not much instant healing taking place when in theta brain waves. However when your brain is just entering theta, it is called rapid eye movement or (REM) also known as the dream state. Most people go through this state rapidly and do not remember or witness the healing benefits. However, just when you are entering theta brain waves at 7.83 Hz, time stands still and great healing can occur.

7.4   Alpha Brain Waves

Alpha brain waves are from 8 to 12 Hz. When you are in alpha brain waves, you are in contact with your subconscious mind and healing can occur rapidly. Alpha brain waves occur when you are in meditation or they can occur in group prayer. Research done by Dr. Elmer Green has shown that the most rapid healing takes place at the alpha-theta transfer, or more precisely, at 7.83 Hz. Dr. Green was formerly the director of research at the Menninger Foundation and the doctor that conducted the energy research on Jack Schwarz. He believes that if you can keep the body at the alpha/theta transfer remarkable healing can occur. If you read my book *Healing Light* you will learn that mode 2 of the Q Laser is programmed at 7.83 Hz and puts the brain in alpha brain waves quickly without any effort on your part. Just turn it on and place it in contact with your head for one three minute cycle.

7.5 Beta Brain Waves

Beta brain waves are from 12 to 26 Hz. This is the conscious brain state – the thinking, talking, listening state. At these frequencies the body is being torn down and no healing or regeneration is taking place. Most people are either in this state, beta, or are in theta the sleep state and they never get into alpha where healing occurs.

7.6 Gamma Brain Waves

Gamma brain waves or what some call super beta, are from 26 and up. Some in the sports world refer to this as the "zone." Others like Jack Schwarz, who are able to access these higher brain frequencies, are able to do unusual and remarkable things. Jack was able to voluntarily elevate his brain frequencies to 60 Hz, which is the same frequency that radios, projectors and other kitchen equipment operate on and instantly shut down that equipment. The Menninger Foundation researched the effect that sexually explicit pictures might have on the human brain by having volunteers watch various sexually explicit multiple media while attached to EEGs, EKGs and blood pressure cuff. There were ten doctors along with Jack and a Yogi Rumanin involved in this research project. Jack and Yogi were late arriving and the other doctors had already begun simultaneously watching eighth or nine different sexual films and slide shows. The back door of the darkened room opened and Jack and Yogi entered. Within minutes one, then two, then three and four projects shut down. Schwartz found sexually explicit scenes vulgar and elevated his frequency to 60 Hz, cancelled the frequency of the projectors and shut them down. Schwarz also demonstrated several times his ability to access higher brain waves with increased voltage generated through excitement to stop bleeding after pushing a large needle through his arm. Schwarz taught that accessing healing frequencies with increased voltage by increasing his excitement level was the secret to instant healing.

It is known that animals operate at higher frequencies than humans. This phenomenon is well demonstrated in the movie *Horse Whisperer*, and in the video, *Dog Whisperer*. It is a fact that like frequencies attract. Positive attracts positive and negative attracts negative. Lynn Grabhorn in her book, *Excuse Me, Your Life Is Waiting*, elaborates on positive versus negative to change your life. Buddy Frumpker in his book, *Test and Grow Healthy*, shows how negative charges produce negative energy and block homeostasis.

The activity in human brains is not due to neurotransmitters as much as it is due to the coherence of brain waves. The neurons of animals' brains are not that much different that those of the human brain – even the fly has similar neurotransmitters.

The ability of the human mind arises not from neurons but from the coherence of brain waves. The coherence of activity in brain waves increases with more powerful brains. This research in an article entitled, *Beyond the Neuron Doctrine*, by Douglas Fields published in June/July 2006, *Scientific American Mind*, sheds light on why low powered resonating lasers that produce a coherent light are so beneficial to the brain.

The brain is an observer and a processor of thoughts attracted from the universe. Be ware of what you attract.

Today in the spiritual world, the buzz word to wellness and   happiness is consciousness. Consciousness means different things to different people but T.S. Elliot may have summed it up best when he said:

Where is the life we have lost in the living?
Where is the wisdom we have lost in the knowledge?
Where is the knowledge we have lost in the information?

7.7 Meditation

One of the hardest things to learn to do is to meditate – to put the mind in neutral – to not think. There are many techniques taught on mediation. Most teachers tell you to get in a comfortable position - listen to some peaceful rhythmic music – get in a peaceful place where water is splashing – birds are singing. When most of us get into that place – we fall asleep. That is not meditation. Meditation is putting the mind in neutral or alpha brain waves - not thinking but also not sleeping. Beneficial mediation then is controlling the brain waves.

7.8 Why Meditate?

Meditation, as used in this book, is a practical guide to utilizing the total mind to achieve total abundance. Aryeh Kaplan, in his magnificent book, *Jewish Meditation: A Practical Guide*, poignantly sums up why we should meditate and what we can achieve by applied active meditation.

He first states that you might find yourself thinking about such fundamental questions as:

What do I ultimately want out of life?

What gives life meaning?

What is the meaning of life in general?

If I had my life to live over, what would I do with it? What ideals, if any, would I be willing to die for? What would bring me more happiness than anything else in the world?

To these questions, Rabbi Kaplan answers, "As you explore what is most meaningful to you, you may come to a point where you feel that you are reaching a new threshold. You may find yourself pondering not only the meaning of your own life, but the very meaning of existence in general. At this point, you will have discovered God."

Rabbi Kaplan concludes, "Once a person discovers God in this manner, he might want to transform his meditation into a conversation with God. If one discovers God as the ultimate depth of one's being, then the way to relate to this depth would be to relate to God. At this point one's meditation on the meaning of existence might become a silent conversation with God."

Applied active meditation is the most effective known method of interacting with the Universal Mind and bringing its powers into your mind and self. With daily applied active meditation, you can put the enormous wisdom, insight and power of the Universal Mind to use in your personal life. Remember that the emphasis in applied active meditation is on the process rather than on the specific goal. When you set a specific goal and focus on that goal alone, you limit what you can achieve. When you focus on the process, instead, your possible achievements are virtually unlimited. Focus on the process. You will almost invariably achieve your goal; and you will go beyond that goal to achieve successes that you have not yet dreamed of. Goals are limited to your past experiences. The process can take you to the new, the unexpected, and the extraordinary.

All the aspects of applied active meditation are based on the principle that our universe and everything in it, including us, are composed of and controlled by electromagnetic radiation. This is the carrier of the Universal Mind and its intelligence. How we make use of this Universal Mind and the intelligence it contains determines how successful and rewarding our lives will be. It determines how we grow and evolve and what each one of us becomes during our lifetime. The greater the electromagnetic energy available for our use, the greater our power will be to achieve whatever we wish.

A simple, easy to learn type of meditation that can be practiced any where, regardless of the noise, the confusion or the stress, is merely to count your breath. It can and should be practiced when you are in a stressful situation – in doctors' offices – in dental offices – in hospitals - in airports – traffic jams or when work and family conditions become stressful.

7.9   Practice Counting Your Breath

It works this way. Empty all the air from your lungs, consciously slowly breathe in - feel the cool air entering through your nose. Start to count the numeral "one" – just thinking it – not out loud, think just the first syllable or sound – the "won" sound. Then more slowly than you inhaled, slowly exhale. Feel the warm air going out through the nose and while exhaling, complete the one count with a "nnn." Repeat this process – try to even the breathing rhythms by exhaling twice as slowly as you inhale while continuing to repeat the numeral "one" in a long drawn out "wwwooooonnnnn." In some cultures this would be called a mantra. The fact is that even though thoughts can pop in and out of the brain in milli-seconds, the brain cannot think of two things at once, so when you are breathing deeply while counting; it puts the brain in alpha waves – your peaceful brain waves. TRY IT NOW – it is easy and it works. Remember to use it any time you are in a stressful situation – even if you only use it for a few minutes at a time , it will be beneficial.

Chapter 8

MIND

The mind is in you, around you, and of you and extends well beyond you. It creates your SOUL

—Dr Larry Lytle

8.1   The Power of the Total Mind

Your mind is the conduit between yourself and the Universal Mind. It is also the connection between your eternal self and your physical body. Through the use of your total mind, you can achieve your life's purpose, which is to bring the power of the Universal Mind to your eternal self.

When I talk about your total mind, I am referring to a tripartite entity. You may not be fully aware of these three distinctly different functions: the conscious, the paraconscious and the subconscious. Your conscious mind communicates with the material world. Your paraconscious mind communicates with the Universal Mind. Your subconscious mind stores all the information from both the material world and the Universal Mind —then combines this information into your plans, dreams, desires, awareness and the eventual actions you take.

8.2   Abundance through the Universal Mind

An abundant life comes through contact and interaction with the Universal Mind. When you add the unlimited power of the Universal Mind to your personal self, you achieve the means to abundance.

What is the Universal Mind? How do we know it exists? According to what laws does it operate?

What I am calling the Universal Mind has the power to put together atoms, then molecules and, finally, the unique living form that is you. Universal energy built the entire universe and is responsible for keeping it functioning. You are built by the Universal Mind and you are kept alive and functioning by universal intelligence. The power of the Universal Mind can be converted to your own personal power. It is the greatest source of power available to you on earth, when you use it in your life,

Despite all that modern physics has demonstrated about the creative energy that operates in the world, western society persists in emphasizing the material at the expense of the non-material. You have been taught to rely on your physical senses as your only source of information, that unless you can weigh or measure something, it doesn't exist. You have been taught you are nothing more than your physical body and that, as an individual material being, you are separate from all other people, animals and objects in the universe.

In accordance with the law of universal harmony, the energy you radiate will determine the level of universal intelligence you can contact, and therefore bring back to your subconscious mind. Your brain waves are a precise indicator of the quality of energy you are radiating. The longer the wave and the higher the amplitude, the more powerful the universal intelligence you contact.

The best instrument on earth that can tune into these longest waves and bring to you the incredible universal intelligence they contain is your paraconscious mind! The next best instrument is a precise low level laser which will be discussed later. When your mind is producing predominantly theta and delta brain waves, it is maximally tuning into universal power and intelligence. When your brain is predominantly in delta and operating at 1 cycle per second (cps), you are sending out brain waves 186,282 miles long. These longest waves vibrate with the greatest portion of the Universal Mind. Each brain wave you send out returns with intelligence from the Universal Mind for your use. When you add the voltage of high excitement to the longest brain waves, you have the best of all conditions for tuning into universal intelligence.

However, the universal intelligence in your subconscious mind must be directly experienced before it can become a part of you and be of any value. The only way you can experience it is to act on it by putting it to use in your daily life. Only when you take action and creatively experience the universal intelligence in your own life does it become a permanent part of your self.

8.3   Speed of Light

This relationship is explained by the simple equation: (x) = the speed of light—or 186,282 miles per second. Maxwell showed that all electromagnetic waves travel at the speed of light. Therefore for any electromagnetic wave, the number of vibrations taking place each second, times the wavelength, must equal 186,282 miles. Thus the higher the frequency as measured in cycles per second, the shorter the wavelength—and conversely—the lower the frequency, the greater the wavelength.

For example, if the frequency is 10,000 cycles per second, then 10,000 times the wavelength is 186,282 miles. Dividing the speed of light by the frequency of 10,000 cycles per second gives a wavelength of 18.6282 miles. At a frequency of 1,000 cycles per second, you have a wavelength of 186.282 miles. At 1 cycle per second, which is a delta brain wave emission, each wave is 186,282 miles long!

In our physical world waves of a certain length carry pictures into our TV sets. Even longer ones carry sounds and words and ideas.

A radio antenna attracts those waves carrying sounds, and a radio transforms them to within human auditory range.

The higher the frequency and the shorter the wavelength, the greater the kinetic or physical power the wave will be. At high frequencies, electromagnetic waves can cut through steel. Longer waves have little physical power but carry huge amounts of universal intelligence. To communicate best with this intelligence, we use the longer waves.

The Universal Mind is the intelligence that designed and created the universe and is now operating it. The universe functions in accordance with strict laws. Nothing occurs by chance. You, yourself are the best proof of the existence of the Universal Mind. You are made-up of approximately 72 trillion cells that work together to keep you functioning. Each of these parts is a complete factory in itself, far more complex than any computer or instrument humans have managed to build. Each cell performs over one million chemical reactions every second. Each cell has to interact perfectly with the other 72 trillion cells during these millions of reactions per second. For your cells to operate as a unit requires incredible intelligence. Where does this intelligence come from, and how is it communicated and carried?

What can I tell you about the Universal Mind? I can explain that it is everywhere, surrounding you completely and moving within you. Until now you have been severely limited in your ability to perceive the Universal Mind. If you follow the meditation and psycho/physical exercises in this book, you will expand your perception. You will learn how to use every part of your mind and to express its power in your life. Through the use of applied active meditation, you will come in contact with the Universal Mind, and incorporate its intelligence into your daily life.

I mentioned before there are three parts of your mind, the conscious, the subconscious and the paraconscious. The mind and how it works or doesn't work plays a major part in your health and wellness. The mind isn't just in your head. It fills, surrounds, and extends well beyond your body. It is a known fact that your belief system limits awareness and can affect your health and well-being. "Soul-size" your affairs and make peace with death and it is not hard to achieve peace and wellness.

8.4   The Conscious Mind

Your conscious mind is what you think and depends on the five physical senses for its basic information. It is the part that is in contact with the material world. With its thinking and reasoning powers, your conscious mind produces words to describe what your five physical senses are telling it. The reasoning power of your conscious mind is what makes you human. This power is both your greatest distinction and the worst obstacle to the fulfillment of your life's purpose. Depending on the rational mind alone leads to a perception of separateness and isolation. Ego is a product of your conscious mind, and it creates the perception that you are an individual entity, separate from all else in the universe.

Each day your conscious mind is bombarded with millions of stimuli. If your conscious mind tried to respond to, or even be aware of most of these stimuli, you would not survive. The onslaught would be too great. When this torrent of sensations hits the conscious mind, it has to decide which to allow in and which to block out.

Your conscious mind acts according to belief systems you formulated based upon what you were told and taught when you were in the womb and growing up. Your teachings and learning come from your grandparents, parents, teachers, friends, news media, clans, gangs, church, and governments, and the laws they make. This information is acted upon by your conscious mind and your subconscious stores all the information brought to it and fits that information into patterns that define your way of looking at the world. Once these patterns are in place, your conscious mind chooses to see and experience only those stimuli and ideas that correspond to and reinforce your trained belief systems. Your conscious mind reflects what you believe and is your reality and your truth of the world as you see it. It guides your actions according to your belief systems that control it – a scary scenario especially since many of your teachers may have been wrong.

8.5   The Subconscious Mind

The subconscious mind functions as the archives or library of your total self. All the input from the conscious mind is permanently registered here. The subconscious mind then forms relationships between the contents of these archives and develops plans of action and reaction. This means, whenever you want to do anything, your subconscious mind takes information from its archives and sends instructions to the conscious mind on what to do, how to do it and how to feel about it. Your conscious and subconscious minds work as a team. Stimulus A enters your conscious mind. You respond with B. Therefore stimulus A is paired with response B in your subconscious archives. When your conscious mind next encounters stimulus A, your subconscious mind will prompt you to respond with B.

From your subconscious archives comes your instruction book on life. The cards you have in this file determine the wideness or narrowness of the life you live, its success or failure, its health or disease, its misery or bliss.

For most people, the belief systems put together in the subconscious mind build a prison, limiting awareness and shutting out possibilities. Their experiences are similar to the voluntary confinement of flies that have been in a jar with a lid on it. Once these flies have tried to get out of the jar and encountered the lid enough times, they give up. Even when the lid is removed, most of the flies will remain in the jar. Based on their experience of hitting the lid, the flies reduce the size of their reality to the confines of the jar. Most people have constructed lids over their lives.

The same phenomenon has been demonstrated with fish. Put fish in a large tank and in the middle of the tank place a piece of glass separating the two halves. After a number of days, remove the glass. Most of the fish will continue to live in only their half of the tank.

There have been more sophisticated studies done about the limitations that the teaming of the conscious and subconscious minds can impose. At Harvard an experiment was done with cats and different kinds of stimuli. One group of kittens was raised in a room that had only horizontal stripes. Another group was raised in a room with only vertical stripes. When the kittens grew up, the horizontal stripe group could not see the vertical legs of a chair that was placed in the room. Examination of these cats' brains showed they did not have the connections between neurons to see vertical stimuli. Likewise, the vertical stripe group could not see horizontal lines; their brains never developed the connections that would have allowed them to detect horizontals.

Studies like the one done at Harvard prove that the mechanics of perception are such that your initial sensory exposures and how you interpret them actually develop a nervous system designed to see only that to which you were exposed in the first place. Research by Candace Pert has shown that each thought creates a specific neurotransmitter which helps to determine how your nervous system will respond and to what it will respond.

Therefore, if you have not been exposed to a specific stimulus, or if it has not been interpreted for you in a certain way, it does not exist for you. The Buddhist law of Maya, which is the law of illusion, speaks of the limitations of perception. Maya does not say that the material world is an illusion. Rather, the illusion is your belief that the small part of universal reality of which you are aware is the whole picture. What you perceive is indeed real, but it is only a small part of reality. It is not the essential reality. Your personal reality is: the lid is still on top of your jar.

Today you have built a model of so-called scientific biology based on the illusion that your world is only made-up of material objects, each one individual and separated from each other in time and space. You are like the Harvard cats, except instead of vertical or horizontal stripes, you use data, measurements and things you call facts to define your reality. You are not wrong. But you are not right either. You do not see the whole picture. So much more is available to you when you learn how to expand your awareness and use your total mind.

The subconscious mind is what you feel - what you feel emotionally and also what you feel inside your body. You may feel strong or experience a powerful energy flow. A part of you may actually feel hot and some parts of you may feel vibrant and healthy. When you have a greater awareness of your feelings, you will also have a greater power to be in control of your life. The subconscious mind really knows all, but the conscious thinking mind keeps it locked up like a prison. Applied kinesiology, that is if the operator is capable or uses techniques to take his/her beliefs and ego out of the equation, works at the subconscious level and can be used by professional and laypeople to seek answers for health and wellness decisions.

8.6   The Paraconscious Mind

This brings us to the third function of the mind; the paraconscious mind, the function that is in contact with the Universal Mind. Paraconscious means beyond the conscious. Society does little to encourage recognition of the paraconscious function. In fact, most of the experts will tell you the paraconscious mind is a delusion. Once you personally experience the paraconscious mind, however, you will know that your mind has three functions. You will know how to use all three of them.

With your paraconscious mind, you can directly experience and communicate with the Universal Mind! This means you can also add universal intelligence to your subconscious archives. The insight and power in the Universal Mind is far, far greater than anything your consciously processed data could add.

When you learn to recognize your paraconscious mind and to acknowledge that through it you are in touch with the Universal Mind you will experience a quantum increase in power and effectiveness. By adding the input of your paraconscious mind to that of your conscious mind, your life will attain new dimensions. Your possibilities will become virtually unlimited!

8.7   Measuring the Mind's Functions

Scientific evidence for the three functions of the mind comes from the measurement of the electrical impulses produced by the brain. As the live brain functions, its nerve cells generate electrical impulses. These impulses are emitted as waves, and this electrical activity can be measured.

Two measurements can be made of each brain wave. First is frequency, which determines the length of brain waves and is measured in cycles per second (cps). The lower the frequency, the fewer cycles per second, the longer the brain wave would be.

Secondly, we can measure the strength or power of each wave. We do this in terms of amplitude or the height of each wave. The more powerful a brain wave, the greater its amplitude or height will be. The amplitude of brain waves is measured in micro volts.

The different types of brain waves correspond to different functions of the mind. The conscious mind expresses it self through beta waves. The subconscious mind expresses itself through alpha waves. The paraconscious mind produces both theta and delta waves.

8.8   Two Paraconscious Functions

The Universal Mind has a much greater intelligence than your conscious mind. The Universal Mind brings information and insights that are not available to the conscious mind. Almost every one of you has experienced this. In today's psychology, delta is called deep sleep, and theta is called pre-sleep.

How many times have you consciously tried to solve a problem for hours with no results? You go to sleep. Your conscious mind is no longer at work, but your paraconscious mind is. You wake up suddenly at 5 A.M. with the answer. (A great deal of the answers to how I developed the Q Laser system came to me in this manner).

One of the most famous examples of this is how Thomas Edison invented the electric light bulb. He tried repeatedly to find a filament that would not burn up when he heated it enough to produce light.

Then one night in his sleep, with his conscious mind turned off, his paraconscious mind was able to show him charcoal being made. Reportedly, he immediately saw the answer to his problem. The process that makes charcoal from coal keeps the available oxygen low so that the coal doesn't burn up. Edison removed the oxygen from the light bulb, and the heated filament glowed and gave light for eight hours before burning up.

The light bulb was invented by the paraconscious input of Thomas Edison.

Your conscious mind, which is strongly verbal in all its images and experiences, has a direct line to your subconscious archives. That line is far stronger than the line from your paraconscious mind. Therefore, as long as you are using the input of your conscious mind, you cannot receive paraconscious information. Thus to add the intelligence of the Universal Mind to your archives, you must shut down your conscious input and tune in to your paraconscious mind.

8.9   Action: an Essential Connection

Adding the intelligence of the Universal Mind to the archives of your subconscious is only the first connection on what is called the circuit of self-empowerment. The essential second connection is spontaneous action in accordance with this new input. Unless you act on the new input from the Universal Mind, it will pass through and be gone. You must act rapidly on the paraconscious input without letting in the questions and doubts of the conscious mind.

Keep your journal or a pen and paper by your bed and when you awaken with a new thought, write it down regardless of the time of the night. Another option is to keep a digital recorder by your bedside and record your thoughts as they happen

As already pointed out, your actions are controlled by your conscious mind. So when the intelligence of the Universal Mind comes to the subconscious mind, the subconscious mind prompts the conscious mind to act. Doubts or fears in the conscious mind will immediately stop all paraconscious input.

8.10 Excitement: Energy in Motion

In order to act immediately and spontaneously, you have to have power, which is another quantifiable aspect of your mind. Power is the micro voltage your brain produces.

The average person walking around in beta is operating with a micro voltage of 5 to 15. In alpha, theta or delta, the micro voltage is up between 45 and 55. However, for the paraconscious input to overcome the doubts and fears of the conscious mind and to spur it into creative action, the micro voltage has to be between 85 and 95.

How do you get your micro voltage up? It flies when you totally desire something, when you become consumed with excitement. To transform universal power into personal power, you need excitement. Excitement is energy in motion. "E"- motion or getting excited is the greatest wealth you can have on this earth. Through sustained excitement, you have the power to add the intelligence of the Universal Mind to your subconscious archives.

As you go through this program and learn to use your total mind power, you will gain a sense of excitement that will give you the push needed to keep moving, changing, and evolving. You will feel more alive and more aware than you have ever felt before.

8.11 The Circuit of Self-empowerment

The increase in power that you will experience is cumulative; it flows along a circuit that spirals ever upwards. First, your conscious mind is continually sending input from your daily life into your subconscious. Your paraconscious mind tunes into the Universal Mind and deposits information from the Universal Mind into your subconscious mind. Your subconscious mind then integrates the intelligence from the Universal Mind with the input of daily events and undergoes an immense increase in power. The subconscious mind uses its new strength and awareness to draw up plans for action in your daily life. The conscious mind now must put those plans into action without doubts, fears or changes in any way. Then the actions you take are much wiser and more powerful because of the integration that has occurred. And when you take action, the power of the Universal Mind becomes your own personal power. And so the upward spiral goes.

This continuous movement to higher levels is the circuit of self- empowerment. It has four basic connections which are:

1. Conscious mind input from your daily life

2. Paraconscious mind input from the Universal Mind

3. Formulation of plans in the subconscious mind

4. Action taken on those plans. (The action must be that devised by the paraconscious-subconscious mind interaction—without any changes by the doubts, fears, and belief systems of the conscious mind.) Too many people spend most of their thinking time worrying about or talking about their aches, pains illnesses, lab tests, past or planned surgeries. These thoughts and words are negative. Don't do that! Follow the advice in *Energy Transcendence* and turn the negative into positive. You will be healthier and happier.

At the end of each circuit, two things occur. First, the new power brought to you from the Universal Mind becomes a permanent part of you and is yours to use, whenever needed, for the rest of your life. This increased personal power is at your disposal each time you face new problems or have new desires you wish to achieve. There is no known limit to the personal power that you can accumulate. Every time you use your total mind, you increase your personal power. Whatever you add to your subconscious archives is there permanently. You never lose what you add because evolution is a one-way street. You can fail to use what is available to you, but you can never lose it.

The second thing that occurs is that once the circuit of self- empowerment is completed a new bit of the Universal Mind is added to your eternal self. Completing a circuit elevates your eternal self to a higher level. Whatever you gain from the Universal Mind is yours forever. When the time comes for your body to cease functioning, you will take nothing material with you. But you will take all the intelligence from the Universal Mind that you have accumulated. The question for your trip on earth is: How much of the Universal Mind are you going to add to your eternal self?

8.12   Learning Total Mind Power

You have the power to ensure that your eternal self—that individualized creative energy package which has separated from the Universal Mind to become you—will leave your material body at a much more evolved level than when your body was born.

As a human being, you have been given the ability to tune into the intelligence and power of the universe, to live side by side with your creator. To refuse to use this gift is to turn your back on your creator. To ignore this remarkable ability is to miss the purpose of life. You have been put on this earth to evolve, to move with the Universal Mind in its quest for growth and change. You can fulfill your earthly task only by learning to use your total mind. Only through the use of your total mind can you achieve the evolution that your eternal self and the universe require. Your practice of applied active meditation is not meant to be a limited, isolated segment of your daily life. It is a complete meditation that becomes a constant part of your everyday activities.

To achieve these goals via meditation, it takes practice and discipline. Remember, the first rewards are mere glimpses of the vast power you are beginning to tap into. The best is always yet to come.

Through meditation exercises, you will learn:

1.   How to use all the functions of your mind

2.   How to greatly increase the power of your mind

3.   And finally, how to use your total mind power in daily life to achieve abundance

Knowledge becomes valuable only when you build a model with it, and use that model to take action. Your model becomes valid only with successful use. Having a map is no substitute for actually walking the territory.

8.13 Ways the Mind Communicates

The mind communicates in many ways. Mind to mind is considered telepathy. Mind to environment is psychokinesis (PK) and mind to objects is clairvoyance. Experiments involving random number generators (RNGs) demonstrate that the mind can control the outcome of throwing dice.

Mind to mind communication has been demonstrated by the ganzfeld state. The ganzfeld state is achieved by placing halved ping pong balls over the eyes of the receiver while he/she is keeping the eyes open and simultaneously shining a red light into them and at the same time covering the ears with headphones playing white sound.

Clairvoyance is the art of seeing beyond the five senses. Clairvoyance is often called the "sixth sense" or extra sensory perception (ESP). It is related to the images that are always present in our minds that bring messages from other frequency and realms. Clairvoyance is used exclusively to refer to the transfer of information that is both contemporary to, and hidden from, the individual said to be receiving it. In clairvoyance we see with what is commonly called the third eye. Clairvoyance was first demonstrated in 1890 by the sister of Hans Berger who sensed her brother was in danger and sent a telegram to her father asking him to go warn her brother. Because of the warning, Berger survived the danger and went on to develop the first electroencephalogram (EEG)

Many people do not know that the neuropeptides which play a role in how your brain works are made in the gut. The term "gut feelings" or intuition describes your mind's communication with the gut to give immediate directions for the cells lining the gut to release various neuropeptides into the blood stream for immediate use by the brain.

While biology is the study of all life; energy is the underlying substance of all life. Bioenergetics is the study of the flow and transformation of energy in and between living organisms and between living organisms and their environment. John Oschman in *Energy Medicine: The Scientific Basis of Bioenergy Therapies* states that our DNA responds to pulsing magnetic fields and describes an extra cellular matrix that has multifaceted relationship to energy fields and exerts just as much influence on cellular dynamics as hormones and neurotransmitters. Bioenergetics is the study of how cellular metabolism such as choice of fuel, energy production and storage and consumption governs the interaction between cells. Bioenergetics is quite diverse and depends a great deal on photons.

8.14 Biofeedback

Active meditation is powerful because it can give you access to the Universal Mind without the filter of conscious thought. You don't have to experience something first in the physical world for it to be real to your paraconscious mind. This opens the whole world of universal intelligence and power to you.

Up until now you have been conditioned to let your conscious mind predominate in the way you function. Almost everything in your subconscious mind was put there by your conscious mind alone and, thus, came only from the material world available to your five physical senses. As long as the input to your subconscious mind is determined by your conscious mind, the input from your paraconscious mind to your subconscious mind will be completely blocked, or too weak to be of use.

For paraconscious input to the subconscious mind to be strong enough to be usable, the overwhelming input from the conscious mind must be stopped or greatly reduced. Then, and only then, can the paraconscious input gain access to the subconscious storehouse with sufficient power for awareness and usage.

But the conscious mind does have an important role to play in increasing your personal power. If the paraconscious mind rules to the exclusion of the conscious mind, no action can be taken on the paraconscious input. The conscious mind is required for universal intelligence to be put into action. Paraconscious input will stay locked away in the subconscious archives until the conscious mind uses it to act creatively. Once the action is taken, another circuit of self-empowerment is completed.

Knowing comes only from experience. Knowing occurs when your paraconscious mind brings intelligence from the Universal Mind into your subconscious mind—which, in turn, integrates this new information with all the input that has preceded it. The subconscious mind then presents new and more powerful plans of action to your conscious mind. And your conscious mind puts these plans to work in your daily life. The result is the circuit of self-empowerment, one of the most powerful processes available to any human being. By the act of writing this down you are putting intelligence from the Universal Mind to work in your daily life.

Research has shown that mentally experiencing an activity can affect the body the same way as actual performance of it. Early research was conducted on muscles alone and used biofeedback instruments. People sat in comfortable chairs and visualized a series of physical exercises. Their muscles did not move. Nevertheless, the biofeedback instruments registered the same during the visualization as they did during actual physical exercise

8.15 Thought

If, in the beginning, the universe was created by God as light and all things are light – including thought. So it stands that a thought is just energy. But where does a thought come from? How is it that two people can have a thought at the same time, thousands of miles apart? If it is true that the human brain is the only brain that can think, how do other animals communicate such as proven in the hundredth monkey research? *The Hundredth Monkey* is an old story where two teams of researchers were studying monkeys in the Atlantic and Pacific Ocean islands, a half world apart. They observed that the monkeys were having trouble eating their sweet potatoes because of the sand on them. One day one of the monkeys ran to the ocean and washed the sand off his sweet potato. The rest of the monkeys in his family immediately followed and washed the sand off their sweet potatoes. Amazingly half way around the World in another ocean, it was observed that another family of monkeys washed sand off their sweet potatoes at exactly the same time. Then it was observed that one hundred monkeys in each ocean followed suit and from then on it seems that all monkeys washed the sand off their sweet potatoes before eating them. This is an old story that demonstrates that energy is "non local" It is everywhere at once. A thought is out there for the taking. Just keep your mind open and your antennae up and you will be pleased with the thoughts that are attracted to your brain for processing.

Subtle thoughts limit wellness. It is believed that stress is externally caused and it is to blame for much of your illness. You will learn that is not true! Do you remember the term psychoneuroendocrineimmunology – that is the way you think affects your neurological system, which in turn affects our endocrine system, which affects your immune system? Watch what and how you think. Avoid fear. In this day and age of degenerative diseases, "The Worst Thing You Can Have Done May Be A Diagnosis" – that is unless you know before hand what you are going to do with the diagnosis if it is negative or positive.

It is no mystery – how you think or react to events controls your physiological body processes and affects your health and everything you do. In fact, there is empirical evidence from experiments done on random number generators that the mind can control physical process from a distance – i.e. prayer.

So if thoughts produce energy which affects your health, wellness and disease, then it is obvious that you need to learn to control your thinking.

Chapter 9

USING PSYCHO-PHYSICAL REHERSAL FOR ENERGY TRANSCENDENCE

True change and higher human adaptation are not made by resistance to old habits. Change is not a matter of not doing something; it is a matter of doing something else.

—Da Avabhasa (Da Free John)

9.1 Introduction to Psycho-Physical Rehearsal

More research has shown that all areas of performance benefit from visualization. By experiencing something mentally, you can affect the results you will achieve when you actually take action. You can mentally rehearse anything: the way your body moves, the way your emotions run and the way your thoughts precede.

The idea of psycho-physical rehearsal is to experience something prior to its actual happening. Any kind of experience—physical, emotional or mental—is appropriate for psycho-physical rehearsal.

Psycho-physical rehearsal applies to anything you would like to become an expert at—to have full capacity at. You will be using your total mind, and will actually experience, probably for the first time in your life, achievement of whatever you desire. Psycho-physical rehearsal is your method for discovering potential and developing the ability to achieve a total and full life.

Psycho-physical rehearsal has been used extensively and successfully in sports. The popular term for this is the "inner game" of tennis, golf, football, etc. All these inner games do the sport first in a mental state in order to improve physical actions before using them. You can use psycho-physical rehearsal to dramatically improve your potential for any situation in which you expect to find yourself.

It can be done almost anywhere and at any time. You don't need to withdraw from humankind. You can perform your normal activities at the same time you are applying the technique. Once learned, psycho-physical rehearsal allows you to gain direct access to intelligence from the Universal Mind and transform it into your own personal power—at will. Whenever you use this technique to transcend a problem or obtain a desire, you not only meet your immediate goal, you also increase your inner resources for future use.

9.2 The Basic Steps of Energy Transcendence Using Psycho-Physical Rehearsal

1. Set up your horizon in your mind and project the current situation onto it.

2. Stop conscious input by becoming an observer. Send your second self into the scene. Keep yourself outside the scene as an observer, not adding any conscious input.

3. Observe the occurrences on the horizon. This is input from your paraconscious mind.

4. Take the actions you have observed and apply them immediately to the situation you're in.

5. You now have completed a circuit of self-empowerment.

6. You now get an immediate response to your psycho-physical rehearsal. Being immediate it is the most wonderful feedback you can get on how effective your rehearsal was.

As you can see, the psycho-physical rehearsal is a way to make creative intelligence from the Universal Mind a constant part of your daily life. You do not limit meditation to an hour in a chair at the end of the day. With psycho-physical rehearsal, you use meditation, your paraconscious mind and universal creative intelligence all day, everyday. Psycho-physical rehearsal gives you the ability to add universal power to your life any time you need or desire it. It is one of the greatest sources of power known. It is a one-way street to abundance.

9.3   More Power for the Future

The process for applying psycho-physical rehearsal to upcoming events has similar steps. Let's take the example of an important meeting that is scheduled for tomorrow. Use your conscious mind to project the meeting room onto your horizon. Insert your second self into that room. Initially direct your second self to experience the room itself. Does anything feel uncomfortable? Let your second self work to alleviate the discomfort.

Experience the people in the room individually, then as a group. Next experience the material you wish to present and discuss, and finally what actions will take place, and how universal intelligence can lead you to the results you most desire.

Remember that the input from your conscious mind is at an end once the scene is put on your horizon. You then watch what happens. You are an observer. You do not enter the scene. Watch your second self, which is acting according to intelligence from the Universal Mind. When the scene has played out, use your journal to record your observations.

On the day of the meeting, you will feel at ease. You have been here before and you know what to do. You will be taking into that meeting the actions and insights suggested by the Universal Mind. Due to your use of psycho-physical rehearsal, you will have the highest intelligence and power in the universe as your partner for the meeting.

89

You always have the option of doing another psycho-physical rehearsal during the meeting. Thus as the meeting progresses, you can continue to add intelligence from the Universal Mind. As different situations arise, universal power will be there to help you by adding its ideas, suggestions and insights to your subconscious mind.

Do you have worries, doubts and fears about the upcoming meeting? What better way to transcend them than in a psycho- physical rehearsal before the actual meeting. Rather than reacting to these worries, fears and doubts you have replaced them with high excitement, high expectation and high anticipation. When you combine universal intelligence with excitement and confidence, there is no better script for success.

9.4   Steps for Future Psycho-physical Rehearsal

Whenever you complete a psycho-physical rehearsal, your body radiates energy back into the surrounding universe. This energy then vibrates with and brings back to you the universal energy with which it is in harmony. The more powerful your radiation, the more powerful the universal intelligence it will bring you.

In general, the psycho-physical rehearsal of the future consists of five separate but totally related psycho-physical rehearsals. In the first your second self responds to the environment. It makes any changes necessary, so the environment becomes comfortable to your second self. By creating a comfortable environment, your second self goes into the second psycho-physical rehearsal.

Your second self now looks at and interacts individually with each of the people you believe will be there. Respond to each of them as you believe them to be, never as you wish them to be. You can also add people, real or fictional, who will be annoying to you or supporting of you. By so doing you can see how universal intelligence would respond to your projected annoyances and supports. You will now be prepared to respond to whatever occurs with the power and wisdom of universal intelligence at your side.

Now follow with a psycho-physical rehearsal of the individual people, of your second self interacting with the entire group. At the completion of that, the next psycho-physical rehearsal is on whatever you expect to present at this meeting. What objections and approvals would you anticipate, and how would universal intelligence react to them? Become an observer. Let universal intelligence show you some possible objections or approvals you would never think of. In addition, experience what presentations or actions you might expect from others, and rehearse your response along with that of universal intelligence.

Finally, have your second self respond to the actions that take place at the meeting or whatever environment your psycho-physical rehearsal is in. You now have covered the environment, the individual people, the group collectively, the presentations—plus the responses to them and possible plans of action. You have completed the psycho-physical rehearsal.

If at the end your mind has anything in it other than positive thoughts and success—if you feel anything other than high excitement, anticipation and expectations—you still have not replaced all of your conscious mind's doubts, fears and worries. Redo the psycho-physical rehearsal until you identify them, devalue them, and replace them. You will know when this is so because your mind will be filled only with visions of success; your feelings will be only of high excitement, anticipation and expectation.

9.5   More Power and Radiance

Every living thing radiates energy from itself. Your personal radiation follows the law of universal harmony. It vibrates with those waves of universal intelligence you are in harmony with.

Your personal radiation is like a boomerang. Being born of you, it returns to you. When it returns it brings with it the power of harmonious universal intelligence. The more powerful your radiation, the more powerful the radiation of the Universal Mind it will vibrate with and bring back to you!

91

Each complete psycho-physical rehearsal cycle increases both the personal power you have available and the power of your next radiation. Each day you become more powerful and more radiant. You are evolving.

You will never arrive at a final destination. You may achieve specific results, but you will always be moving on to a higher level of living, whichever one is next for you. Each day of your life, psycho-physical rehearsal offers you the opportunity to become more joined with the universal energy that created you. How wonderful to be aware of this and, by this awareness, to have the opportunity of experiencing it every day of your life!

9.6   Thought Patterns and Psycho-Physical Rehearsal

Psycho-physical rehearsal gives you the power to achieve and do what you previously could not. If you have trouble accomplishing something, your problem probably lies in your attitude toward that thing. You may have been told you were incapable of doing it. You may have tried it once and been less than successful. Your conscious mind now tells you that you are incapable of doing it—that you are not good enough. You begin to question your capabilities. It holds true that the more you question, the more you doubt, and the more willing you become to listen to the negative input of others.

Most of the time, if there is a specific thing you would like to do or to achieve, you do not spontaneously go after it. Instead, you listen to your conscious mind, which tells you to pause and take a look at how the experts would go about it. Then you begin comparing yourself with these experts. If you have never done the thing before, naturally you will come up short. With any comparison you put yourself in a state of competition. You begin to doubt that you are good enough. If there is anything that can drain your energy, it is this comparison and competition.

You will be much better off when you turn to your paraconscious mind before you even consider looking anywhere else for information on how to proceed. When you receive the input of your paraconscious mind, you become aware of your own inherent qualities and powers. You may perceive some doubts, but you will discover what that doubting is all about. You will usually find that the roots of any doubts you have are based on the opinions of others about your capabilities.

Remember, ours is a bipolar universe, a universe of matching negatives and positives. And when they are joined we create a current and energy flows. For every fear, doubt and worry we have, universal intelligence has powerful visions, excitement and expectations. Remember also -- every time we replace anything inappropriate, our success and powers grow. We become more.

When you use psycho-physical rehearsal to encourage input from your paraconscious mind, three things occur.

First, you become aware of your present doubts and   comparisons and their sources.

Second, you become aware of the inherent powers you have.

Third, you gain new powers from the new paraconscious input.

To do a psycho-physical rehearsal of anything, you must pay attention to the process rather than the outcome. The result you hope to attain is of secondary importance. To begin the process, the first step is to create an environment. Do not assume what that environment should be. If for instance, your goal is to call on the Universal Mind to help you make a painting, you will project your horizon and then find an appropriate environment for painting. A studio may appear. If the furnishings in that studio keep changing shape, go with the changes. Let them happen. It is not unusual for the images in a psycho-physical rehearsal to change. The first image you put up there on your horizon was probably influenced by your conscious mind using the material available from your subconscious mind. Future changes that occur will be from the Universal Mind operating through your paraconscious mind.

The studio you've placed on your horizon may change into an outdoor scene, a beautiful forest with squirrels darting around. The

Universal Mind is showing you the environment in which you can do your best painting. Your initial idea that you would be in a studio to paint was probably based on what authorities told you. You had that notion filed away in your subconscious mind. Your conscious mind went to the file, found the idea about the studio and put it up on the horizon as the proper setting for your psycho-physical rehearsal of painting. Your paraconscious mind, free of the stagnation of belief systems, knows a better environment for you and sends that picture to your subconscious mind.

When you become more experienced at psycho-physical rehearsal, you will often not use your conscious mind to set up the environment. Your paraconscious mind and the Universal Mind will set it up for you from the start.

9.7   The Experience of Non-attachment

Non-attachment is another essential concept in the whole process of applied active meditation. With psycho-physical rehearsal, you can actually experience non-attachment, and thereby know what it feels like and what it is. When you practice achieving non-attachment in the world of the psycho-physical rehearsal, you will be an expert at it when you need it in the world of material reality.

Non-attached does not mean detached. Detached means you do not care, and take no action. If you are non-attached, you care a great deal and you do take action, but your emotions are free to be used in any direction you like. When you are attached, your emotions are directed one way and are not free to change directions. When you become non-attached, your emotions are free to move in whatever direction you feel is most appropriate and productive.

For example, suppose someone does something injurious to you or your family. You hate that person with a vengeance. Your hate is directed at and completely attached to that person. Hate, fear, jealousy and anger are all first cousins and require a great deal of energy – all negative. Since that energy is attached to the person you hate, you are limited in how you can use it. You can use it to try to injure the person you hate. Or if you cannot injure that individual, you can just let it swell up inside of you, leaving little room for positive energy. Retained emotions are an enormous drain of energy. The energy drain of strong repressed emotions makes appropriate actions almost impossible.

When strong emotions are retained, they also affect the functioning of the physical body. Most emotions, and especially fears, first affect the adrenal glands and then the urinary tract, kidneys and colon. Hate, envy and jealousy directly affect the spleen, which is your reserve battery, the reserve power source of your body. Your spleen also draws out iron and produces red blood cells. It is important for the functioning of your immune system. When your immune system is impaired, you are open to disease. So retaining hate, or any of its cousins that produce strong negative emotion, weakens you in almost all functions and increases your susceptibility to disease.

Emotion is energy in motion. When you repress an emotion it de energizes you. You also become attached to repressed emotions and they hold you fast. When you decide not to express an emotion, you rob it of its ability to move and to energize you. You attach it to something that holds it fast. Becoming non-attached is basic for increasing personal power. Your psycho-physical rehearsal is one of the best and most effective training grounds for learning the process of freeing your emotions from debilitating attachments.

Instead of directing your new increase in energy toward hitting the nose of the person you hate, use it to increase your competence at transcending. You use it to increase your ability to respond to any situation. As a result of freeing your energy and using it for self- development, you are a person more in control of yourself than one controlled by negative emotions.

9.8   Reaction versus Response

For almost every occurrence in your life you have two options: you can react or you can respond. Which you choose will determine your success, your achievements and, most important, the quality of your life. The difference between reacting and responding is the difference between using part of your mind and using your total mind. It is also the difference between being attached and being non-attached.

When you react, you direct your emotion toward the situation that provoked the reaction. Whether you react to hate by punching the offending person or using that energy to clean your desk, you are still reacting. Therefore, you are tied to the situation that caused you to hate. Your emotions are not free to flow away from their cause.

When you react, you are operating on assumptions. Reaction occurs when you use only the conscious and subconscious aspects of your mind. With your conscious mind you are aware of, and in contact with, only what is happening in your material life at the present moment. Your conscious mind draws on the archives in your subconscious to interpret occurrences in your life. It is limited to your previous experiences and what you've been taught. To see beyond what you already know, you must use your paraconscious mind.

When you rely exclusively on your conscious-subconscious mind, as events occur, immediately there comes this little image of how you were treated before. You assume you will be treated the same way this time. Then you react to what you assume is happening or about to happen by going into a state of defense. <u>Reaction is always defensive.</u>

When you react to any situation, even so-called good events, you become attached. When you assume a threat and react to it, your entire body chemistry focuses on one set of assumptions. These assumptions have become so enormous; they have so filled your mind that nothing else can enter. You are attached to them. You cannot go beyond them. You are stagnated, and your radiant energy drops to very low levels.

When you live a life of reacting, you are constantly walking around in a state of readiness. Somebody out there is going to take advantage of me—is going to do harm to me—is going to compete with me and defeat me. So you are always fighting, always competing, always in readiness to make the other guy a loser and yourself a winner. The disharmony and damage resulting from such a view injures you and the entire world.

When you walk around in a state of readiness, your muscles, nervous system, brain, and mind all contract and the power of your radiation drops sharply. With such contraction, with such weak energy radiation, you can only know and be aware of what is happening in your immediate local environment. When you are so contracted that your voltage goes down, so does your resistance to outside forces. You become vulnerable to everything from bacteria to disease, from constant fear to a host of mental and emotional problems.

When you respond to a situation, you don't immediately strike out in one direction. Before taking action or making decisions, you stop your conscious mind's input and seek feedback from your paraconscious mind. This way you add universal intelligence and its power to the situation before taking any action. With the addition of such power to your decision-making and actions, you are far more effective and robust than if you're a slave to reaction.

The power and insight you gain from your paraconscious input remains a part of you, for your use whenever needed. By using psycho-physical rehearsal to respond, you transcend your emotion and its original cause, and you move to a higher, more effective plane of living.

When strong emotions arise, they create an abundance of energy. When the energy created is non-attached and free to move, it can be used to transcend the cause of the emotion, and thus increase personal power. This is true of happy and good emotions as well as irritating ones. If you become attached to a joy and want to keep repeating that feeling for the rest of your life, you will be blocking the flow of your energy as much as if you were attached to a negative emotion. You will be limiting yourself to your present happiness, and preventing an inflow of even greater joys.

When you react you are living in a unipolar world. You see only the problem. When you respond you are living in a bipolar world. You see both the problem and its opposite appropriate vision in universal intelligence. You experience the whole picture, taking action to replace the inappropriate problem with an appropriate vision.

Every psycho-physical rehearsal is a response, not a reaction. You are responding to an event that has happened, is occurring presently or will occur. By contacting the Universal Mind and bringing forth its intelligence, you see the bipolar picture and set your energy free to flow in the direction that will bring you the most wisdom and power. Psycho-physical rehearsal develops your ability to experience the bipolar world, to respond to the whole world. It allows you to achieve both non-attachment and spontaneity and, thus, a lifetime of continual personal evolution.

9.9   Repetition, Repetition, Repetition

The place to start practicing non-attachment is within the scene you create for your psycho-physical rehearsal. As you observe the setting of the event you're rehearsing—be it an event occurring in the present or one that will occur—register your responses to everything in that setting. Be aware of your five senses of seeing, hearing, smelling, tasting and feeling. Now notice which ones are stimulated. Get all you can out of your initial observations of the setting. Note your level of comfort or discomfort: those specific aspects that contribute to your comfort and those that contribute to your discomfort. Note if the comfort or discomfort affects your body. What do you feel? Do you experience areas of excitement or areas of blockage? Where are they? When you become proficient with your psycho-physical rehearsals, you can actually discover how your body is physiologically functioning. At this beginning level, however, just tune in to what extent you are aware of your body functions.

Perceive yourself as really being in the environment you have created. You must experience the psycho-physical rehearsal as reality. As soon as you feel you have examined all aspects of the environment and your relationship to it, consciously withdraw.

Note what happens to you during this state of withdrawal. Remove your self from the environment. Then, mentally erase whatever is left of the environment. Become aware of any thoughts now coming to you. Prepare again to focus on the environment and to go back into it.

Why go back into the same environment? Your first trip into an environment is like a scouting expedition. You have to find your way in unfamiliar territory. You have to learn how to adapt. Most people, when they first perceive and experience an unfamiliar environment, feel nervous. This is normal. It's also why you let yourself out of the environment, and then go back for another look. The first time you can miss a lot of things that might hamper you later on. The second time there should be less nervousness because a certain adaptation and familiarization have already occurred.

When the environment occurs again, notice what comes back. See if any changes are already taking place. Are you feeling more familiar with it? Now again put yourself into it. Explore by moving around. Focus on the details. See if you can find any new details since your last visit. You may discover some more things that make you uncomfortable. The situation was new the first time, and you were so nervous you did not realize some other discomfort.

When you feel disturbed by what you encounter, continue to familiarize yourself with it until you see how to handle it. Then get away from it and go back again, and see how well you handle it this time. Is it still disturbing, or can you now handle it and move on? This is a further step in your non-attachment training. When you cannot handle it, you are attached to it. When you become non- attached, you allow in the power to handle it.

This non-attachment can occur quite rapidly. You can adapt quickly once you feel the environment is not as threatening as it seemed in the first encounter.

9.10 Using Psycho-Physical Rehearsal to Transcend Fear

A marvelous and supportive environment will not teach you how to handle your fears and anxieties. Psycho-physical rehearsal allows you to encounter your fears and anxieties, so they lose their power over you. You free all the emotion trapped in attachment to particulars, and you become stronger.

Fear produces a paralyzing effect. Most people have a lot of fears. But remember fears can be used in psycho-physical rehearsal to grow and evolve. Every time you experience a fear, it is a challenge to do something about it. Almost invariably, once you have faced your fear, you will realize it was not totally valid to begin with. With psycho-physical rehearsal, rather than push fear away and try to avoid it, you respond to and transcend it and, thus, use it to build your personal power. Rather than reacting, you respond to your fear by tuning into the Universal Mind. Then, let your paraconscious bring intelligence from the Universal Mind into your subconscious. You complete the circuit by taking the action directed by your conscious mind, staying with your fear until all its negative effects have been overcome by your increased personal power.

Through the psycho-physical rehearsal you learn to see the bipolar universe you live in. When you see an inappropriate action in our daily life, at the same time you see a clear vision of an appropriate action in the Universal Mind. When you join the two together in your mind, you produce a tremendous creative power. This creative power, with great intensity, now seeks expression in the world of your daily life. Use this power. When you use it you transform it into your own personal power, and then you have the power to successfully handle almost any environment you ever encounter.

9.11 Facing a Hostile Environment

Right away you probably hoped to find a nice environment that was suitable for your pursuits. Please don't expect this from the psycho-physical rehearsal. If you're like most people, you have made enormous efforts in your life to change everything and everybody in your environment so it is safe and suitable for you. You have the crazy idea the world should be set up according to your desires. If the environment is hostile, you're not going to blame yourself for not being able to handle it. You are going to blame it and the people connected with it. They are causing your problems, not you. And you are going to try to change them. You are also going to try to change whatever else in your environment is at the root of your disease.

But the point of psycho-physical rehearsal is to make changes in yourself so you become capable of living well in any environment. It is fine to say, hey, this is not the best environment and I want to see it improved. The greatest improvement will come, however, when you change yourself so you can handle that environment. First, go to work on familiarizing yourself with that environment as it is, so you will not be fixated on what is causing you trouble. Then allow your paraconscious mind to bring universal intelligence to bear on the environment.

9.12 The Experience of Spontaneity

One of the most important benefits of the psycho-physical rehearsal is learning to take immediate and spontaneous action on the intelligence from the Universal Mind that your paraconscious mind brings you. Doing psycho-physical rehearsals trains you to stop the conscious mind's interfering input and allow the paraconscious mind to function.

9.13 Access to a Great Source of Information

The late great Napoleon Hill, whose writings and research on success have helped so many, stated that the major difference between a genius and the average person is not that the genius is more brilliant or more educated. The difference, according to Dr. Hill, is the genius has access to a source of information and intelligence that the average person does not. Dr. Hill called this source of information infinite intelligence. We call it Universal Mind.

The Universal Mind has direction. It is creative. Each time you complete a psycho-physical rehearsal cycle, you add creative intelligence to your present intelligence. This increases your level of consciousness, your inner resources and your power. Thus, with the completion of each psycho-physical rehearsal cycle, you create a new you with greater power and intelligence than existed before.

For example, suppose you desire more financial success. Psycho-physical rehearsal will help you to design and put into action a plan for achieving this. Suppose you wish to run your business more effectively. Psycho-physical rehearsal will put you in contact with the Universal Mind, which will, after it is transformed into your own personal intelligence, help you to design your plan of action for achieving a higher level of effectiveness. Suppose you are a sales rep. There is no greater sales tool than applying psycho-physical rehearsal to each specific sales situation before and during its actual occurrence.

In the complex area of human relationships, psycho-physical rehearsal can build bridges rather than walls, can move you toward cooperation and away from conflict. It can even help build love.

With psycho-physical rehearsal, you will learn to add intelligence from the Universal Mind to whatever is occurring in your life right now. With each subsequent psycho-physical rehearsal, you will learn to add intelligence from the Universal Mind for the future events in your life.

With this psycho-physical rehearsal, you add intelligence from the Universal Mind to whatever you are doing at the time you are doing it. You draw on the Universal Mind to give direction to the situation in which you find yourself.

Via active meditation you can dramatically change your life and attract new knowledge that your subconscious mind has processed and fed into a plan of action. You then can identify your plan and act on it.

You do not do your psycho-physical rehearsal in your head. It is very important that you project the actions outside yourself. Your created horizon will always be within your energy field. When you increase your radiance and power with psycho-physical rehearsals, you will experience your horizon moving farther away from you. This indicates that you are increasing your energy field, and hence your energy and power.

Where is your mind? Understanding the answer to this question is basic for psycho-physical rehearsal. Remember, you cannot truly understand the answers until you experience them. While I am now sharing knowledge with you, you will have true understanding only from your own experience. You will gain that experience by doing the cosmic review and psycho-physical rehearsals and putting your new powers into action.

The mind is within and without: It surrounds the body. It is the mediator, the link between the body and the Universal Mind. It communicates with both. However, the mind is also within. Its energy extends to every cell in the body. Therefore we have the oft- repeated statement from Jack Schwarz: "All of your body is in your mind, but not all of your mind is in your body."

During psycho-physical rehearsal you are in touch with the mind, not just the brain. The brain is comparable to an amplifier. It magnifies the intelligence brought to it by the mind. It also transforms the energy from the mind into the biochemicals your body needs for life. When the power of universal intelligence activates the mind, the brain will produce the biochemicals of bodily health. When the universal intelligence inflow is blocked, the brain usually produces the biochemicals of disease. When you wish to add universal intelligence and power to whatever you are currently doing, practice psycho-physical rehearsal. Begin by first projecting a horizon and then project yourself onto that horizon and apply whatever is occurring in your life and resolve it with universal intelligence.

While you remain active in your current situation, you stop all conscious mind input from entering the scene occurring on your horizon. You observe what is happening on your horizon and what your second self is doing.

The actions occurring on your horizon are those that the Universal Mind is suggesting for you to take in your current situation. Spontaneously act on the suggestions from the Universal Mind. Do not hesitate. Allow no doubts, questions or fears. You will feel excitement, faith and high energy.

Since you are applying input from the Universal Mind immediately in your daily life, you will get immediate feedback on how effective your psycho-physical rehearsal is. Even though you achieve some success the first time you do this, remember you will achieve greater success each time you call on the psycho-physical rehearsal, even in this same situation. Each time you do, your power and success increase.

When you first begin your meditations you will attain your weakest results. As you increase your personal power, the power of your results greatly increases. But you must start at the beginning and take your first steps. Only then can you learn to sprint.

If ever you get nothing on your horizon or when the results from applying what you do get are unsuccessful, you know that you were not yet ready for the step you tried to take. You need more preparation. Go back, take a look and discover what fears, belief systems and attachments are preventing you from progressing. Once you've removed these energy blocks and raised your consciousness, you will get successful results with your psycho-physical rehearsal.

The intelligence from the Universal Mind will bring you the vision and power needed to transcend the negative feelings. As is true with so much in life, you cannot change the thing, but you can increase your power to the point where the thing no longer offends or disturbs you. You are now in control rather than being controlled.

You will find the psycho-physical rehearsal useful almost every day of your life. Now is the time to start.

9.14 Plan of Action

Another way to get your mind in a state of relaxation/meditation is to practice breathing rhythms or merely count your breath.

However, if that form does not suit your purposes, ignore it and design your own way of keeping track of what you experience. The important thing is to record the thoughts and feelings you were aware of as you watched the events of a day unfold. What thoughts and actions struck you as appropriate; what ones seemed inappropriate? What new thoughts did you have once you had run through a complete cosmic review? Did you strengthen your appropriate thoughts? Did you devalue and transcend your inappropriate thoughts and actions?

Follow a similar line of questioning with your feelings. What feelings were you aware of? Did you notice any fears? Which feelings seemed appropriate, and which inappropriate? What new appropriate feelings did you have at the conclusion of your cosmic review? Did you strengthen your appropriate feelings and devalue your inappropriate feelings? Did you become aware of your blocking belief systems and your energizing belief systems?

After you have written about your thoughts and feelings during the cosmic review, you can write about the actions you viewed. What actions did you take during the day that was appropriate? What actions were inappropriate? What new actions were suggested to you by your cosmic review? Most important, how do you plan to implement your new power in your daily life?

Applied active meditation achieves its results by multiplying the effects of your circuits of self-empowerment. The impact is cumulative. Each time you use the process, its momentum increases. It will soon become autonomous—self-generating and self-directing. Through applied active meditation and the use of your journal, you continually grow. You move closer to being one with the Universal Mind, the force that created you. You become the co-creator of your life. And your life becomes bliss.

Chapter 10

BREATHING

And the Lord God formed man of the dust of the ground, and breathed into his nostrils the breath of life; and man became a living soul.
                                                    GENESIS 2 -Verse7

10.1 Introduction

The efficiency of our physical, mental, emotional and spiritual functions are enhanced or weakened by the manner in which we breathe. Your general health and well being will be enhanced by effective breathing. It's a must for maximum results.

Your life is dependent on breathing. You can exist for some time without eating and for a shorter time without drinking, but not much longer than seven minutes without breathing. Breathing affects your vitality and health. It plays a major role in realigning mind and body. It can help you do away with fear and its cousins, worry, hate and anger. It is an effective, easy, cheap, drug free way of way of eliminating stress and other emotional problems. Effective breathing can help unfold the latent powers within you. If you do not breathe right, no matter how diligent you are otherwise in implementing the processes presented here, your increase in personal power will be limited.

This chapter will teach you how to breathe effectively. There are six levels of breathing

1. High breathing or clavicular

2. Mid-breathing or intercostal

3. Low breathing or diaphragmatic

4. The complete breath

5. Full breathing or pelvic

6. Correct breathing or paradoxical

10.2   Level 1—High Breathing

High breathing is called clavicular because when you breathe this way, you raise your clavicle, or collarbone, in short, abrupt movements. If you ask someone to take a deep breath and their shoulders raise, they are either high or intercostal breathers. Unfortunately most people, unless they have been trained otherwise are high or shallow breathers. This very fast, shallow breathing expands your lungs hardly at all, filling only the top part of the lungs to about one-eighth capacity. High breathing typically occurs when you are in a panic. Since your lungs are not filled, your blood does not get enough oxygen to distribute throughout your body. You can feel weak and paralyzed. Your brain uses twenty percent of the oxygen in your blood. When you panic, you have difficulty thinking clearly. High breathing under any conditions interferes with your flow of thoughts. It causes thought paralysis because not enough oxygen is getting to the brain. When the brain gets enough oxygen and sugar, which are its nutrients, it strengthens and activates the hippocampus, the area of the brain that activates the five physical senses. What the senses perceive then goes to the part of the brain called the thalamus, which edits information not pertaining to the particular state you are in. The rest is sent to the pituitary gland. The pituitary gland then synthesizes this information, and based on what it says, activates all of the glands of your endocrine system, including the adrenal glands, which in turn activate your gonadal system. The gonadal system is the energy source for your entire body. It activates the pancreas and the liver. Your liver produces sugar that is immediately regulated by insulin from your pancreas. That sugar supplies your whole body with strength and energy.

The whole physiological process depends upon having that main fuel, oxygen, at adequate levels in the brain. Therefore, the more you fill your lungs, the better off you are. A brain that is operating with very little oxygen produces a high frequency of beta brain waves, with low amplitude. This means that the brain has little capacity for radiating energy.

10.3   Level 2—Mid-Breathing

Mid-breathing is also called intercostal because it expands the chest and ribs. The muscles in between the ribs are the intercostal muscles. If you use the middle portion of your rib cage to breathe, you can expand your lungs more fully—to approximately twenty-five percent capacity. While mid-breathing also produces beta brain waves, it's more effective than high breathing. It provides enough oxygen to keep body and brain functioning, but at low levels. Mid-breathing is the predominant pattern in western civilization. It is the kind of breathing that encourages submission to outside authority rather than taking control of your own life.

10.4   Level 3—Low Breathing

Low breathing originates in the diaphragm, a partition of muscles and tendons between the chest and abdominal cavities. With diaphragmatic breathing, the lungs are five-eighths full, and the brain predominantly functions in alpha.

As you will recall, the alpha brain wave is associated with the subconscious part of the mind that regulates all bodily functions. With low breathing, your subconscious mind works the way it should and automatically regulates physiological functions. Neither high nor mid-breathing activate the subconscious mind and the autonomic nervous system does not function the way it should. Your body gets out of balance.

Learning to breathe from the diaphragm is the first step to correct breathing. Take a moment to feel how your body moves when you breathe from your diaphragm. When you inhale, your abdomen will expand and your lower ribs lift. Your chest will remain stationary. Place one hand on your abdomen and the other hand on your chest. Now inhale. If you are using your diaphragm, the hand on your abdomen should move out while the hand on your chest does not move. Practice this until you can do it with ease.

By breathing from your diaphragm, you pull the air down into the lungs. The farther down your diaphragm moves, the more your lungs fill with air. Once you can breathe this way easily, you can begin to develop a rhythm. Inhale for a count of 8 with each count being approximately one second. Hold your breath for a count of 8. Exhale for a count of 8. Hold out for a count of 4. Repeat the sequence: Inhale for 8, hold for 8, exhale for 8 and hold for 4. With rhythmic, diaphragmatic breathing, you are beginning to train your body to become aware of and establish effective breathing patterns.

10.5   Level 4---The Complete Breath

Once diaphragmatic breathing becomes natural for you, you are ready to progress to complete breathing. The complete breath begins with the diaphragm. Inhale as you do when practicing low breathing. Once you have completed the inhale, move your breath up to fill the middle part of your lungs, pushing out your lower ribs, breastbone and chest. You will feel pressure around your ribs as you do this. Keep the breath moving and fill the top of your lungs. You upper chest will expand and your upper ribs lift. Your abdomen will be slightly drawn in to support your filling lungs.

Try placing your hands on your abdomen and chest so you can feel the movement of each part of your body. Your abdomen expands on the inhale. Then your chest begins to enlarge as you move the air up to the top of your lungs.

Now exhale slowly, letting your breath out twice as slow as you took it in. In all these breathing exercises, you will discover that the slower the exhalation, the greater its power. As you exhale, hold your chest in a firm position and draw your abdomen in a little, slowly lifting it upwards as the air leaves your lungs. When the air is exhaled, relax your chest and abdomen. With a little practice, the complete breath will become almost automatic.

With the complete breath, all parts of your respiratory system are exercised. It combines the low, middle and high breaths, moving rapidly from one level to the next forming one continuous breath. The complete breath has an alpha rhythm and works to keep the subconscious mind on track.

10.6 Level 5—Full Breathing

Once you've mastered the complete breath technique, your breathing can be stretched to an even greater level of effectiveness through practice of the full breath, or the pelvic breath. At this level of breathing, instead of just lifting your lower ribs, you draw your diaphragm even deeper. When you inhale, your whole pelvis expands—not just the abdominal portion. Begin by drawing your diaphragm down. Keep doing so until you feel your pelvis beginning to extend. Then go into the rest of the stages of the complete breath by moving the air up into your lungs. Feel your chest expand.

The full breath fills your lungs nearly completely and supplies maximum oxygen to your brain. Through it, you activate the autonomic nervous system and your whole lower intestinal area, which is your gonadic or generative system, the energy source for your entire body. It is your butane tank; the oxygen is your pilot light. When you inhale, you inspire. One meaning of the word inspire is to set on fire.

And the oxygen in the gonadic system sets your entire generative energy on fire.

Most diseases first show their signs in the abdominal area. But the brain is the place where disease actually starts. The brain without sufficient oxygen and energy loses its capacity to regulate body function. Full breathing keeps the generative process and its energy flowing. It also keeps the flow even, so you don't go from tremendous energy highs to devastating lows.

10.7 Level 6—Correct Breathing

The sixth level of breathing, the most powerful of all, is the so- called paradoxical or reverse breathing. The Tibetan masters of breathing call this correct breathing. Some of you will find it unnatural. It requires conscious effort, produces tension and does not become automatic. Only Yoga or Tibetan masters should use this type of breathing. It is not a natural way for most people to breath.

In diaphragmatic breathing, your abdomen extends as you inhale. In paradoxical breathing, your abdomen pulls inward as you inhale. You will feel the air moving strongly throughout your entire pelvic area. You may experience the feel of oxygen entering your gonadic system.

When you inhale paradoxically, there will be a hollow point in your abdomen. The Tibetans train themselves so they can walk around with a football in the hollow of their abdomen. The football stays put as long as they don't exhale. The moment they exhale, the belly plunges back, and out pops the ball—with a lot of power.

The training that paradoxical breathing requires gives you great control over your intestinal area and gonadic system. If this level of breathing seems to be too difficult for you, do not despair. Most of us have had no experience at all in this kind of breathing. Knowing that it is a possibility may be enough. Practicing it from time to time may also suffice.

For you to make progress in this book, the most important level of breathing is level four, the complete breath. Be sure you have mastered it before you proceed to the breathing rhythms that follow. The complete breath combines the first three levels of breathing and fills your lungs. Whether you inhale by pushing your diaphragm down and extending your abdomen (low breathing), by thrusting your pelvis out (full breathing) or by collapsing your abdomen (paradoxical breathing), you must fill your lungs to the top before you begin to exhale. Once you can do this, you will be receptive to the rest of the exercises in this book.

10.8   Breathing Rhythms and States of Consciousness

Aside from these different levels of breathing, there are different rhythms of breathing. You practiced one rhythm—8, 8, 8, 4—when you first tried breathing from the diaphragm. The important thing about rhythms is they are directly linked to different levels of consciousness. Ground breaking experiments on Jack Schwarz, the author of *Human Energy Systems*, done at the Menninger Clinic and the Langley Porter Neuropsychiatric Institute, demonstrated that breathing rhythms can alter the state of consciousness.

Jack had the ability to produce different brain wave states—beta, alpha, delta or theta—on command. He knew what each different state feels like, and he could duplicate that feeling whenever he chose to. Before the experiments, he did not know exactly how he moved from state to state. Researchers wanted to figure out the mechanics behind his amazing ability. They used sophisticated instruments to measure Jack's physiological processes as he changed from one state to another. After many measurements, scientists found only one variable as Jack moved from one brain wave state to the next: his breathing rhythm. Whenever he was asked to go to a different brain wave frequency, Jack changed the pattern of his breathing.

Researchers at the Menninger Foundation recorded his breathing rhythms and then tested a large number of people, asking them to breathe as he had. In every case, a specific breathing rhythm produced the same brain wave activity. This pioneering research is extremely exciting because it means all of us can move into any state of consciousness we desire if we know the breathing rhythm associated with that state!

You too can learn these life changing breathing rhythms. In the following exercises, you will consciously move yourself into specific brain wave states by altering the rhythm of your breathing. The purpose of these exercises is to show you what each brain wave state feels like. Once you know the feeling, you will be able to move into that state whenever you wish.

Use these exercises to increase your awareness of how you breathe during various circumstances in your life. If a certain rhythm is not helpful in a particular situation, you have the power to change it. After you concentrate on your breathing rhythms for a time, your subconscious mind will take control and automatically change the rhythm to put you into the most appropriate state for whatever situation you're in.

10.9 Breathing Exercises

In the breathing pattern exercises you are about to do, keep track of what happens. Write down what you experience physically and emotionally in each state of consciousness. The goal of the exercises is to become aware of what each state feels like to you.

In these exercises you will be given counts. For example, inhale for a count of 8. Each count is approximately one second. So inhaling for a count of 8 is inhaling for approximately eight seconds.

To be effective, your breathing must be either diaphragmatic or pelvic. Before beginning the exercises, be sure you can easily breathe diaphragmatically and/or pelvically. To get maximum oxygen to the brain, inhale through both nostrils and exhale through the nose.

Some breathing techniques recommend exhaling through the mouth, however Yogis have discovered that you have tiny fibrils in the nostrils that when stimulated with a slow, prolonged exhalation, activate the parasympathetic division of your autonomic nervous system, so why not take advantage of this phenomena. In the animal world hoofed animals like horses and bulls exhale through their nose. Most of you have seen pictures of the bull in the bull fighting arena with his nostrils wide getting ready to charge the bull fighter. When the bull has given up and near death, only then does he breathe through his mouth.

To warm up for the start of the exercises, practice breathing rhythmically. Breathe in for a count of 8. Hold the breath in for the same count. Exhale for the same count. Then wait for a count of four. Repeat: Inhale for 8, hold for 8, exhale for 8, wait for 4.

Once you can comfortably breathe diaphragmatically and/or pelvically and rhythmically you are ready to begin your exercises. You must learn to do these patterns not only sitting comfortably at home, but at all times and in all situations during your daily life.

10.10 Beta Breathing

Beta breathing is the breathing most people do all day long. When you are not concentrating on your breathing, you tend to breathe at the clavicular or intercostal level. It is very important, however, in all of the exercises that you use only the diaphragmatic or pelvic full breath. You never use clavicular or intercostal breathing in any exercise. This will not give you the oxygen you need for awareness. The point of the exercise is to become acquainted with the rhythm of beta breathing, which is 4, 4, 4, 4. Concentrate on the way this rhythm feels.

Begin now. Always use the diaphragmatic or pelvic complete breath.

Inhale for four seconds: 1, 2, 3, 4.

Hold in the breath for four seconds: 1, 2, 3, 4.

Exhale for four seconds: 1, 2, 3, 4.

Wait for four seconds: 1, 2, 3, 4.

By breathing in the beta rhythm, you concentrate your energy in the conscious function of your mind. No matter how deep your breathing, if the rhythm is 4, 4, 4, 4, the conscious mind will be predominant.

10.11 Alpha Breathing

Alpha brain waves are associated with the functioning of your subconscious mind. Thus when alpha waves are dominant, you are mainly using your subconscious mind. As we have discussed, the subconscious mind regulates your body functions and stores all your experiences. It relates all that is happening to you in the present to your past experiences. Pain control takes place in the alpha state so if you have any pain, always practice alpha breathing. When you are in alpha, you will feel relaxed without feeling drowsy.

The pattern for alpha is 8, 8, 8, 4.

To practice the alpha rhythm, inhale for eight seconds: 1, 2, 3, 4, 5, 6, 7, 8.

Hold your breath for eight counts: 1, 2, 3, 4, 5, 6, 7, 8. Exhale: 1, 2, 3, 4, 5, 6, 7, 8.

Wait: 1, 2, 3, 4.

The waiting count helps to keep your rhythm even. If you find you need oxygen after you have exhaled—if you can't wait comfortably for 4 counts—you had better look to restoring your whole breathing pattern. Make sure you are doing complete breathing. Waiting only four seconds should be effortless.

10.12 The Alpha-Theta Transfer

The key to your ability to change brain wave states at will is recognition of what the different states feel like. At this point in your development of breathing rhythms, an intermediate step—the transfer from alpha to theta—will help you increase your awareness of the differences in the two states. It also introduces a more effective inhale, one that you will always use to change your state of consciousness to the paraconscious.

The alpha-theta transfer pattern is 4, 8, 8, 4.

The 8 count in the previous exercise was a mild inhalation. Now the inhalation is to a more forceful 4 count. This is a faster and more vigorous inhalation. You have to take in the same amount of oxygen during a 4 count that you previously did in an 8 count.

Breathe in from the diaphragm or pelvis: 1, 2, 3, 4.

Hold in the breath: 1, 2, 3, 4, 5, 6, 7, 8.

Exhale: 1, 2, 3, 4, 5, 6, 7, 8.

Wait: 1, 2, 3, 4.

Once you are comfortable with this pattern, you can move to the next exercise.

10.13 Theta Breathing

Theta brain waves are associated with the paraconscious mind. When you are predominately in theta, you are going from your physical ego, your "I" self, into relations with your non-physical, eternal self. Thus in theta you are bringing into your mind information, intelligence and happenings that you cannot experience in the material world. This is the first level of connection that you make with the non-physical universe surrounding you and out of which you are created. It is also the first connection you make with your eternal self. The theta pattern is 4, 8, 16, 4.

Note that it is the exhalation that is changed. You will be exhaling for a longer count than in the previous exercise. Try it. Breathe in from the diaphragm or pelvis: 1, 2, 3, 4.

Hold in: 1, 2, 3, 4, 5, 6, 7, 8.

Exhale: 1, 2, 3, 4, 5, 6, 7, 8, 9, 10, 11, 12, 13, 14, 15, 16.

Wait: 1, 2, 3, 4.

Keep breathing in the theta rhythm until you can comfortably do it. Notice how you feel when your breath moves this way. Be sure you are thoroughly familiar with the theta state before you move on to the next level. If at any time you tend to fall asleep during this exercise, go back and practice the previous breathing rhythm.

10.14 Delta Breathing

Delta brain waves put you into the deepest possible contact with subtle universal energies. It is a difficult exercise and if you can not do it – don't despair – you will be fine with the other breathing rhythms. When in your waking daily life, if you use delta brain waves, you will receive information about the nature of the universe, about infinity itself.

The delta pattern is 4, 8, 32, 4.

Once again, the change is in the length of your exhalation. At this level, you need to be careful not to let too much breath out too early.

Breathe in vigorously from the diaphragm or pelvis: 1, 2, 3, 4.

Hold in: 1, 2, 3, 4, 5, 6, 7, 8.

Exhale: 1, 2, 3, 4, 5, 6, 7, 8, 9, 10, 11, 12, 13, 14, 15, 16, 17, 18, 19, 20, 21, 22, 23, 24, 25, 26, 27, 28, 29, 30, 31, 32.

Wait: 1, 2, 3, 4.

For those of you who ran out of breath before 32, this analogy might help. Compare your exhalation to a trip through a desert. The desert stretches from point A to point B. I'm going to be your guide on this trip, and I advise you to take along a bottle of water. The water has to last from point A to point B. Do not gulp it. When you feel thirsty, just wet your lips and distribute the water very carefully. If you do this, you will arrive at point B without thirst and even with some water left in the bottle.

Try the delta pattern again, being more careful this time with the amount of breath you expend as you exhale. Practice until delta breathing is comfortable for you.

10.15 A Combination Exercise

Once you are familiar with each of the separate states, you are ready for the final exercise, which is to integrate them all. Take your time and go carefully through this exercise, noting the changes in the way you feel as you move from alpha to theta to delta.

First, do three alpha rhythms: 8, 8, 8, 4.

Next, do three alpha-theta transfers: 4, 8, 8, 4.

Be aware of how the transfer feels.

Now do two alpha rhythms (8, 8, 8, 4) and one theta (4, 8, 16, 4).

How does each feel to you? Keep notes.

Finally, you are ready to go all the way into delta. Do two alpha rhythms (8, 8, 8, 4), one theta (4, 8, 16, 4) and one delta (4, 8, 32, 4).

When you go into the paraconscious theta and delta states, your physiological functions are on automatic pilot. Your body remains perfectly regulated while you explore deeper levels of the Universal Mind.

Think of the physiological functions of your body as an engine. The alpha state is the fuel that runs this engine. The engine is located in the corpus callosum area of the brain. Jack Schwarz's studies demonstrate that the moment a person moves into theta, both hemispheres of the brain start to operate in a very balanced way. But the corpus callosum remains in alpha and continues to regulate our body functions. Strong alpha waves have been measured in the corpus callosum when the predominant brain wave state is theta or delta.

On automatic pilot, your body functions on its own. You can turn all your attention toward the information coming in through your theta or delta level.

10.16 Breathing and Repression of Feelings

As you learn the steps toward applied active meditation, you will discover the value of effective breathing. For now, however, I want you to consider using these breathing techniques to help you express your emotions more fully.

The major cause of physical, mental and emotional malfunctions is repressed emotion. Emotion is energy in motion. When emotions are repressed, the flow of energy is stopped. When you repress your emotions, you prevent your energy from being expressed. When energy flow is blocked, both your body and your self will malfunction. You experience an increase in tension. You tire easily and often feel frustrated.

Through breathing, you set energy free. Particularly when you are in the higher states of consciousness, your subconscious mind regulates all the physiological functions of your body to their maximum. As a result, you increase the energy flow to every activity of your life. You'll find that when you are continuously breathing effectively, you will be more expressive. As you go into theta and delta states, you won't hold back as much. You will express more. And you will find yourself more in balance.

10.17 The Right Breathing Pattern for You

Different situations require different breathing patterns. You can apply a simple test to determine whether you are breathing in a way beneficial to you. If you feel increasingly relaxed and at ease, you are using the proper pattern. For instance, you might be driving your car when someone pulls out in front of you. You have to swerve to avoid hitting the other car. If you immediately feel anger which is one of the energy- blocking emotions, you would choose a breathing pattern that will release anger and tension. Let the energy flow easily through you. Consciously practice until your breathing becomes automatic – this may take months. You are looking for the pattern that gives you the greatest energy flow and adds the most to your strength and power. You want to feel the greatest relaxation. As your relaxation increases, so will your excitement! After awhile, your subconscious mind will take control of your breathing and automatically produce the pattern that's best for each situation.

10.18 The Excitement Factor

Using your breathing to produce specific brain waves and to move from one state of consciousness to another will have little benefit if the amplitude or voltage of the brain waves you are producing is low. With low power, changing brain wave frequency is meaningless. High power must accompany whatever brain wave frequency you choose if you want that frequency to be effective. When the frequency is effective it will transfer to you the information, the understanding and the power you need to achieve whatever you desire.

Excitement is the greatest source of power available to you. Please take the word excitement literally. By definition, to excite is to call to activity and to energize. And this is exactly what excitement does to your brain waves—it increases their activity and amplitude.

A high level of excitement also stirs up the chemistry in your body so it can set free energy that has been trapped. Your body is made- up of molecules. These molecules are bundles of bound-together atoms. The binding force is energy. More specifically, the binding force is the energy relinquished by ions, which are atoms that have an electrical charge. Ions fuse together to form molecules. In the fusion, the electrical charge of the ions is given over to the holding together of the molecule. Thus every molecule in your body is filled with energy waiting to be released. We know from splitting the atom how much trapped energy there is to be released.

The power you produce and radiate is the direct consequence of the energy you allow to enter your body and move freely within it.

High energy production makes you almost immune to both disease and failure! Obviously it is of basic and extreme importance to understand what you can do to free your energy and what you do that keeps it trapped.

A major cause of imprisoned energy is questioning or negative thinking. Will they like me or not? Will I be accepted or not? What if? Will this work out as I want it to, or will I fail? Am I smart enough to do this? Do I have the ability to succeed in this or not? Am I good enough? What fears do I have? Fears imprison and stop the flow of almost all energy. According to the famous positive thinker, Napoleon Hill, the six basic fears are, in descending order of importance: poverty, criticism, ill health, lost love, old age and death.

Every book that purports to be a recipe for success has one main ingredient—positive thinking. Every course on how to get rich, how to improve your health, how to find true love will exhort you to increase your excitement level and decrease your fears and doubts. To do this, you must have desire, faith, high expectations and the ability to use your total mind. The combination of these ingredients will send your voltage sky high. You will then operate at a high level of power.

Another element you need to understand in this whole issue of excitement is spontaneity. When your excitement is high, you act spontaneously. You do not allow doubt to enter your mind. You do not allow fears to paralyze you. When you act immediately and spontaneously, you will feel the flow of energy. Don't be afraid. Don't worry about having to conserve your energy. You can remain at a high level of excitement indefinitely!

Excitement brings great energy into your body. It breaks open those molecules and liberates the energy from them. With each breath you take, feel the increase in your powers, feel the level of your personal radiation rising.

You are creating a circuit, using your excitement and breathing to make a divine connection. You will feel universal power and intelligence flow through you. Your excitement level cannot help but increase as you become aware of this flow and know it is continuous and cumulative. You are adding intelligence from the Universal Mind to your temporal self and to your eternal self, and you are helping the evolution of the universe itself to proceed. This is your circuit of transcendence. It is the bottom line of the process called life. Nothing could be more exciting.

10.19 The Fallacy of Aging

Do you believe you can grow old without aging? There is no question that our bodies age. Most of us think we must lose most—if not all—of our capabilities with the passing years. But I know that everyone can add many productive years to life, years that can be virtually free of disease and pain. If we are aware only of our physical bodies, we can't help but age as we grow older. But when we become aware of our total selves, we can grow older and increase our capabilities with each passing day. The difference depends entirely on the process by which you live.

When you use meditation and psycho-physical rehearsal, you are continuously in contact with the Universal Mind—constantly manifesting its power creatively in your daily life. You are continuously evolving to higher levels of consciousness. Living this process is, in my opinion, the purpose of life.

The success of your life is not determined by how many years your physical body remains alive and functioning. The success of your life is constantly gathering more and more intelligence from the Universal Mind and transforming it into your own personal power. When you live in order to receive intelligence, you will discover that each age gives you a unique situation and environment for your purposes. The intelligence from the Universal Mind that you are capable of processing at age twenty is very different from that at age sixty. Believe me; I've lived through both of them!

At each age, you have the opportunity to expand your awareness and consciousness and become more universally intelligent as a total person. As a consequence, you will be more powerful, even though your kinetic or physical power is decreasing. If you lose physical power each year and gain nothing or very little in universal intelligence and power, you age. You stagnate. You deteriorate. Your body is part of the material world and must, according to the second law of thermodynamics, progress from order to disorder—ending in the final disorder we call death. Aging is a tragedy only when you do not match the increasing disorder of your body with an increasing evolution of your total self. When you do match becoming older with an increasing self-evolution, aging becomes a glorious opportunity to add to your powers!

Psycho-physical rehearsal is a basic life process. It is a way to achieve success and joy on earth while assuring the evolution of your eternal self. Once you learn psycho-physical rehearsal, you can transcend aging. You can replace it with continually greater self- evolution, self-development, and self-fulfillment

Chapter 11

PROPRIOCEPTIVE FEEDBACK TO THE BRAIN AND ITS ROLE IN CONTROLLING THE AUTONOMIC NERVOUS SYTSTEM

Not to know and wanting to know is growth – not to know and not wanting to know is <u>ignorance</u>

– Dr. Larry Lytle

11.1   What is Proprioception?

Proprioception is defined as *"the unconscious perception of movement and spatial orientation arising from stimuli within the body itself"* - and is the body's way of protecting itself. Most people are familiar with the more common types of proprioception – for example, unconsciously pulling your hand away from a hot stove, or quickly and unconsciously lifting your foot if you step on a tack. The most delicate proprioception in your body however, is between your upper and lower front teeth. What you have learned in *Energy Transcendence* up to this point is very valuable, but it has some limitations. It is possible, by hypnosis, to put your mind in a state so you will not feel pain, but if the cause of the pain is not eliminated, you have not really solved the problem. As an example, imagine that you have slammed your finger in the car door. There are many ways to control the pain but obviously the first thing to do is open the car door and eliminate the cause. Very few people are aware that the cause of their pain and health problems is faulty proprioception to the brain due to the relationship of how the lower jaw meets the upper jaw or skull.

11.2   Why Haven't I Heard About Proprioception?

A great deal has been written on "dental proprioception;" much of it, a half century ago. It just has not been taught in our dental schools. There is a great deal known about proprioception in your feet and elsewhere, but the mouth has generally been ignored. Following are just a few notable quotes from prominent writers and researchers about the importance of proprioception.

Drs. Penfield and Rasmussen in *Cerebral Cortex of Man* (McMillan, 1950), state: "over 50% of the brain is devoted to the dental area." These notable neurologists, who published many books on neurology and the brain which were used as text books in medical schools, traced the nerves of the brain back to the oral cavity. Considering that the mandible-maxilla occlusion affects over 50% of the body functions, including motor and sensory actions, blood supply to the brain, and low level electrical feedback to the brain, in order to be healthy, this area must receive more attention.

Price-Pottenger studies have shown that the mandibular/maxillary (upper jaw-lower jaw) relationship in populations consuming mainly refined food diets is altered from birth, causing underdevelopment of the premaxilla. (This is the bone that forms the base of the nose and from which the upper six front teeth erupt) This faulty relationship between the lower jaw and the upper jaw causes the 68 pairs of muscles that regulate the mandibular position to fire in response to proprioceptive feedback. These 136 muscles are supposed to be reciprocally balanced, and able to contract and relax naturally. When they are unable to do so, and become tight, faulty proprioceptive feedback to the brain occurs. Dr Al Fonder called this the dental distress syndrome. When these muscles are not in a state of homeostasis, dental distress syndrome is perpetuated, resulting in reduced blood flow to the brain and pituitary gland.

It is believed that this structural problem is a factor in most diseases. Studies conducted on monkeys by Japanese researcher, Dr. Koshi Miura, demonstrated a breakdown in the neurological function. When the height of their back teeth was ground down on one side and not the other, the monkeys lost the use of the arm on that side where the teeth were cut down and were then unable to climb or swing from trees. When the height of the back teeth was restored, the monkeys normal functioning returned. Miura continued this study on more than 75,000 patients. When the patients' missing or short back teeth were covered with a 10mm high dental template (splint), worn at night, and a 5 mm high template worn during the day, the patients had a 75% improvement of 100 medical parameters.

Dr. Ralph Weiss, DDS, reported that over 90% of the patients in a mental hospital in Oregon had lost either their first or second molars (or both) on one or both sides of their jaws.

Dr. Fonder, author of *The Dental Physician*, states:

"Research has demonstrated that excessive dental distress routinely coexists with a pattern of chronic symptoms that are found throughout all systems of the body. These problems quite routinely normalize when the dental dysfunction is eliminated.

There appears to exist a controlling relationship within the body that puts the dental system into a causative role of symptomatology, where a dysfunctioning dental occlusion (proprioception) creates ill-effects throughout many distant areas of the united body. Fonder has termed this the Dental Distress Syndrome."

Proprioception from the oral area is the main signal to both the thalamus and the hypothalamus; the former controls the cerebellum and posture, and the latter controls the stress mechanism. The cerebellum requires proper information from the 5th cranial nerve, also called the trigeminal or mandibular nerve, in order to proceed with postural adjustment. Thus even small changes in the dental proprioception are easily reflected in the neck, shoulders, arms, lower back, legs and feet.

Dr. Hans Selye, the most recognized expert on stress in the world, wrote in the introduction to *The Dental Distress Syndrome* (Dr. Alfred Fonder, 1977),

"Yet, stress – particularly stress of dental origin – pervades man's life in health and disease…I feel that medicine would benefit most by a closer alliance between members of the medical and dental professions."

11.3 Will Result In Reduced Blood Flow to Your Brain

The arteries that bring blood to and from your brain flow directly through 68 pairs of "dental muscles." When these muscles become tight and constricted due to improper dental proprioception, blood flow to the brain and the pituitary gland – the master gland of the body - is reduced or restricted. When these "dental muscles" tighten up, not only do they act like a tourniquet around your neck, they also pull the lower jaw up and back. This blocks venous drainage from the brain. It does not take a rocket scientist to know that when blood flow to and from the brain is reduced, your mental, dental, and physical health will deteriorate.

11.4 Imbalance between Your Body's Sympathetic (SNS) & Parasympathetic Nervous Systems (PNS)

The loss of posterior teeth (or the loss of height in these teeth) allows the front teeth to touch too soon, which activates the sympathetic nervous system (SNS) and decreases the parasympathetic nervous system (PNS). If the height of the back teeth is increased, then the signal to the PNS, which controls your organ system, functions better. Increasing the height of the back teeth will free the premature contact between the upper and lower front teeth and will decrease the signal to the SNS, reduce your stress and reduce joint dysfunction and structural pain. This phenomenon is not generally well known among professionals, but is described by Dr. Al Fonder as the dental distress syndrome.

Over-stimulation of the SNS and under stimulation of the PNS results in (1) increased body activity, (2) increased stress, (3) high blood pressure, (4) increased heart and breathing rates, and (5) decreased glandular, stomach and intestinal function. These conditions are reversed when the PNS is stimulated.

Under-stimulation of the PNS and an over-stimulated SNS is analogous to putting the brakes on your car while trying to accelerate. Or even worse for some with this condition – the cruise control is stuck in the on position with failing or no brakes.

A balance between the PNS and SNS is necessary for good health.

Chapter 12

TRANSCENDENCE WITH LOW LEVEL LASERS

You cannot unknow what you now know
— Dr Larry Lytle

12.1 Introduction to Lasers

You have learned in *Energy Transcendence* that a pain free, drug free, healthy, happy life is dependent on the proper use of energy which transfers negative, bad energy into positive, good energy.

You have been exposed to, and hopefully are practicing; mediation and breathing techniques that will help you transcend the negative into the positive. Now you will learn about a new easy way of delivering energy back to energy starved cells – low level laser therapy.

Einstein first described lasers in the 1960s. Low level, soft or cold lasers have been used in the US for 45 years for bar code check systems and for fewer years, in laser printing and reading CDs and DVDs. Industry and medicine has used higher power, hot lasers for cutting metal and for various procedures in medicine including lasics eye surgery, but low level lasers are just now coming into their own and taking their place in medicine.

Various wave lengths, powers and types of low level lasers have been used around the world for many years with various levels of effectiveness. However, not all low level lasers are created equal. Most low level lasers are single wave length instruments and, depending on the wave length of the laser light, do not penetrate very deeply or carry very much information. The laser industry, in the effort to get the laser energy deeper into the body, increased the power in hopes they could force the energy deeper into the body. This has not worked very well so you haven't heard much about low level lasers. The new Q Laser System has changed all this by developing a way of combining laser wavelengths and using computers to control the power density and frequency, which makes it possible for the healing energy to flow throughout the body.

12.2   What Are Lasers?

Lasers are really wave lengths of light but a different kind of light than that which lights your room or office. Laser light is coherent and travels in a straight beam until it is absorbed by something. Regular light is non-coherent scattered light. It fills the room rather than traveling in a straight line like laser light. A major difference between regular light emitted from various kinds of light bulbs, including light emitting diodes (LEDs) and laser light is that laser light can carry information and noncoherent light such as LEDs and regular light, cannot.

What information do you want the laser beam to carry? In bar code, it not only carries the price of the item but tracks its contents, how many items are left in inventory, where it was made and much, much more. In laser printing, the laser beam instantly reads the print and pictures and transfers that information to another sheet of paper. In CDs or DVDs, the laser beam picks up the sound from the disc and transfers it to the speakers. Low level lasers are used to guide our airplanes and in the control towers at our airports. Our society and the world has gotten quite used to using low level lasers in many areas of our daily life and if we had to go back to the time when they were not available, it would be very difficult. Our quality of life would not be the same without low level lasers.

The kind of light produced by low level lasers comes from combining different elements in a vacuum and then applying either DC or AC energy to activate and excite the elements which then emit energy. The energy is emitted as a continuous beam of light. Different elements each produce a different color or wave length of light. So far the laser industry is only using a few of our 100 or more elements.

12.3 How Do Low Level Lasers Work?

Low level lasers work at the cell level by either resonating or stimulating the cells. But what is the energy they are using? Subtle energy low level lasers like the Q Laser system re-energize by replacing lost electrons. In a previous chapter you learned how cells communicate from cell to cell with their own light – light made at the cell level. You are made of atoms which in turn are just energy.

You learned that a hydrogen ion is a hydrogen atom (single proton) when it loses its electron and is positively charged. Any atom that gains or loses an electron and becomes either positively or negatively charged is called an ion. Since cells are composed of atoms which are a positive charge surround by a negative charge called electrons, we must be very concerned why the atom and subsequently the cell lose electrons.

While the greatest physicists have not answered that question, we do know that when cells lose energy, you get sick or die. The good news is that with the subtle energy resonating Q Laser, you can restore the lost electrons to the sick and injured cells. You can also use low level lasers to stimulate the meridian network. The rule is you should resonate muscles, organs, and glands with fewer than 5 mw of laser energy, such as with the Q10, Q1000, or Q2000 lasers. You stimulate nerves, bone, joints, tendons, cartilage and ligaments with more energy – that is energy above 5 mw but below 500 mw. The Q

Laser System has the 660 and 808 Enhancer Probes that attach to the Q1000 or Q2000 laser for providing stimulating energy.

Low level lasers work on all cells of all tissue and organs regardless of location and heal in a number of ways; however, the major way they heal is by re-energizing the sick and injured cell membranes. Dr. Bruce Lipton, preeminent cellular biologist, says the cell membrane should be called the cell mem "brain" because it is the brain of the cell. When cell membranes are injured, they lose electrons, and it is not the same cell as before. Electrons are lost in many ways including: leaving the field of gravity for space travel, accidents, necessary or elective surgery, viral, bacterial or fungal infections and aging. When electrons are lost, the cell's ability to take in nutrients is compromised.

Chapter 5 discussed frequency, canceling waves and penetration. Medical research has a bad habit of studying the sick. To try to find a cure for cancer, researchers have studied cancer victims for over 50 years with little to show for their efforts. The same goes for nearly all diseases and disorders. The sick are studied in hopes of finding a germ, a virus, a genetic miscoding and etc. It would make more sense to study those that have been able to heal themselves, such as Jack Schwarz, the author of *Human Energy Systems,* and Yogis.

The Q Laser, the most effective laser on the market has been patterned after the energy of Jack Schwarz. When studying with Jack I said to him: "you are different" and he answered by saying: "No, I am not different, I have just learned to unlock it and you have not – all people have the same ability." Only now do I understand what he was talking about. It has to do with finding and unlocking those special frequencies and delivering them with the correct power to restore energy to every cell. I have done that and now I want to pass it on to you so you too can heal yourself and then assist me in spreading the word about *Energy Transcendence*. My purpose in life is to "make a difference in humankind." The outcome of my efforts has culminated in developing the Q Laser System and writing this book. When you couple this remarkable laser instrument with proprioceptive feedback to the brain and what you are learning in *Energy Transcendence*, there is nothing that is impossible.

12.4 Why Haven't I Heard About Low Level Lasers?

One of the best kept secrets in the world is how effective low level lasers can be, not only in controlling pain, but in many other areas of health and wellbeing. There are several reasons for this.

1. Main stream medicine has not yet endorsed low level laser therapy like they have hotter, cutting types of lasers.

2. Insurance companies are slow to accept and pay for low level laser therapy.

3. Low level lasers are a threat to the economy of the drug and health care industry. They work too well and do not need to be replaced. While a good multiple diode laser system such as the Q Laser System, may cost thousands of dollars on the front end, it will last for years. Most laser companies are offering multi-year warranties. Some of the low level laser diodes used in the bar code check out system (the same type of diode used in the Q Laser) have been in continuous function for over 40 years.

4. Unbiased research money is hard to come by. While there were over 2000 published reports in the late1990s on the effectiveness of low level lasers, most of these studies were done by manufacturers. Even though many of these studies were well run, orthodox scientists have trouble accepting the research. Fortunately that is changing.

5. Unbiased research money is now becoming available through the Alternative Complimentary Medical (ACM) division of the National Institute of Health (NIT). Several studies are already completed and others are underway that show a decisive benefit for using low level lasers. Even the FDA (Food and Drug Administration) is conducting their own low level laser research.

6. There is no Low Level Laser Manufacturing Association to set standards and guidelines, such as in the Automobile Association. This creates a very competitive "who do you believe," marketplace and leaves buyers with a wait and see attitude.

7. While the news media occasionally publishes some scattered news on the success of low level lasers, the media finds negative articles and reports sell more news papers and air time than reporting positive news. Plus, TV stations and newspapers seldom air or publish positive results about any individual lasers unless that company buys advertising and that advertising is just too expensive for most laser companies to afford.

12.5   Where Can I Go To Get Treatment?

While there are many medical doctors, energy doctors, naturopathic doctors, dentists, chiropractors and other health care providers using low level lasers, there is no central list for you to call. When looking for a health care provider the responsibility is on your shoulders. Many health care providers say; "I have a laser." Maybe it is a twenty year old single wave length laser or just a small laser pointer that they are using on acupoints. When treating with light, remember, "all light works at least some of the time." The question remains; if the correct laser or correct combination of lasers with the correct power density and frequency were used, would the results be better? I say yes! In today's market it is pretty much buyer beware.

While you may be introduced to laser treatment at your health care provider's office, it is best to own your own laser equipment. Many conditions need laser treatment every day for one to two weeks and then periodically the rest of your life. It is much more convenient and economical to own your own laser equipment and treat yourself and your family in the comfort of your own home.

Many people buy the laser for one thing – thinking that when they have fixed that complaint, they would not need the laser any longer.

This is not true. Energy transcendence is an ongoing process. There will always be negative events that de-energize the cells. There will always be a need to re-energize those cells. The rule is the sooner you apply the laser after sickness or injury, the quicker the body will heal. Never leave home without your laser.

Bobby was a 12 year old foster child from Nappanee, ID, who broke his neck in a trampoline accident. He was paralyzed from the neck down and had spent 5 years flat on his back. A bus driver who owned his own laser and because of his compassion for Bobby began applying mode 3 of the Q1000 laser to Bobbie's broken neck. He applied the laser for just three minutes, twice a week. Within 2 months Bobby was sitting up in bed writing his homework and within six months he was walking and off to college. Research done by Juanita Anders, a neuroscientist at the Uniformed Services University, the US Military's Medical School, collaborated with Kimberly Brynes, a researcher at Georgetown University, to study induced spinal cord injuries to rats. Their research shows that 5 Mw, 780 nm low level laser diodes can repair damaged spinal cords and enable the once injured rats to walk again. The article goes on to state that Anders and Brynes are not the only ones doing promising research with low level lasers. Researchers around the globe are showing benefits on heart attacks, cancer, organ malfunction, nerve injuries, and internal and external wounds. Dr. Harry Whelan, neurology professor at the Medical College of Wisconsin, has demonstrated the effectiveness of low level lasers for treating serious eye injuries. There is no question; low level laser therapy has arrived. What must be taught now is which lasers, what power, how to use low level lasers and how to deliver the energy deep into the tissue without losing its benefit.

12.6 Where Can I Go To Learn More About Low Level Lasers?

There are two low level laser associations with web sites that publish ongoing information

They are: The World Association of Laser Therapy (WALT) found on the internet at www.WALT.org and the North American Association of Laser Therapy (NALT) found at www.NALT.org.

There are many web sites owned by various companies, each promoting their products. While each will quote their own choice of research to promote their own product, there is still considerable unbiased information on low level lasers. When reading these sites, remember one laser, one wave length will not do everything a combination of wave lengths will do.

APPENDIX 1 - EASY COMBINATION TECHNIQUE

This is the basic exercise of *Energy Transcendence* . It combines the age old proven techniques of breathing rhythms, as taught by Jack Schwarz, with the ancient Hawaiian healing technique called ho'oponopono, and the Q Laser system. This laser system dispenses light frequencies with a modern computerized, multi diode, multi frequency, controlled energy output of the patented Q Laser System.

Ho'oponopono is an ancient Hawaiian code of forgiveness, used to correct the things that went wrong in a person's life. Simply put, ho'oponopono means, "to make right," or "to rectify an error." According to the ancient Hawaiians, error arises from thoughts that are tainted by painful memories from the past. Ho'oponopono offers a way to release the energy of these painful thoughts, or errors, which cause imbalance and disease. Loving yourself is the greatest way to improve yourself, and as you improve yourself, you improve the entire world. Simply put, say to yourself "I love you" and "I'm sorry."

When this technique is combined with breathing rhythms and the special frequencies programmed into the Q Laser system, it is synergistic and very, very powerful. One plus one, plus one is not three, it can be 20 or 30 or more.

This easily combined technique is quick, easy to learn, and is the basis for universal healing. Follow these directions.

1. Sit in a comfortable position

2. Turn on your Q Laser to the breathing rhythm-brain mode and apply it to either temple.

3. Over a period of 4 seconds forcefully inhale using the complete breath technique as explained in Chapter 10.5. During this 4 second period the breathing rhythm-brain mode of your Q Laser will be delivering special frequencies

to the brain. As you inhale, slowly and silently say: "I Love You" (Me)

4. At the end of 4 seconds your laser will beep, signaling you to begin slowly exhaling over an 8 second period. During your exhale, silently say:

"I am soooorrrrryyyyyyyyyyyyy" strung out over the 8 second exhale period.

5. At the end of the 8 second period your laser will again beep signaling you to repeat the process until the laser shuts off at the end of 15 repetitions or 3 minutes.

6. Repeat this exercise daily or as often as needed to heal yourself both physically and mentally.

REFERENCES:

1. *Subtle Energies & Energy Medicine,* Marilyn Schlitz *volume 14*Number 1, pages 1-18

2. *Subtle Energy and Energy Medicine,* vol 16, no. 2;p 13 & 21

3. *Energy Healing, Subtle Energies & Energy Medicine* *Jerry E. Wesch, Volume 14 * Number 1 * pages 61 – 76).

4. *Subtle Energy & Energy Medicine,* David Eichler & Bob Nunley, PhD. vol 16, no 2 pp 49-50

5. *Subtle Energy and Energy Medicine,* David Eichler and Bob Nunley, Abstract vol 16, no 2 pp50

6. *The Elegant Universe,* Brian Greene, Mar 2003

7. *The Elegant Universe,* Brian Greene, Mar 2003

8. *Science and Human Transformations, Subtle Energy and Energy Medicine,* Bill Tiller, vol 16, no. 2

9 *Subtle Energy and energy Medicine,* Maryanne Cowan & Bob Nunley Ph.D, vol 16, no. 2 pp 37-39

10. *Dual Strategy of the Immune Response;* David Lowenfels, Townsend Letter, June 2006; pp *68-75*

11. *Subtle Energy and Energy Medicine,* Maryanne Cowan, Bob Nunley, PhD.,Vol 16, no. 2, pp37-40

OTHER READING AND REFERENCES:

The Body Electric, Robt O. Becker; Morrow NY 1985

Crosscurrents, Robt. O. Becker, Jeremy P. Tarcher, Los Angeles, 1990

Blueprint for Immortality: the Electric Patterns of Life, Neville Spearman, London 1972

Biologically Closed Electrical Circuits B. Nordenstrom, Nordic Stockholm, 1983

Healing Light, Larry Lytle, Authorhouse, 2004

Test and Grow Healthy, Sanford "Buddy" Frumpker, out of print

Mind Map, Sanford "Buddy" Frumpker, out of print

Human Energy Systems, Jack Schwarz, out of print

The Fabric of the Cosmos, Brian Greene, First Vintage Books 2005

Conversations With God book1, Neale Donald Walsch, G.P.Putnam's Sons, NY 1995

Conversations With God book2 , Neale Donald Walsch,Hampton Roads Publishing Co, 1997,

The Power of Now, Eckhart Tolle, Namaste Publishing, Canada, 1999

Biology of Belief, Bruce Lipton c, Mountain of Love/Eleite Books, Santa Rosa, Ca, 2005

The Wisdom of Your Cells,, Bruce Lipton

Conversations With God book1, Neale Donald Walsch, Sounds True audio

Way of the Peaceful Warrior, Dan Millman, New World Library.

NO Ordinary Moments, Dan Millman, New World Library.

Laser Therapy Handbook, Turner and Hode, Prima Books, Sweden

Healing Light DVD Series – 16 hour series: Larry Lytle

Low Level Laser User's Manual; Larry Lytle

Rife Frequencies; Nina Silver

The Universal Healer book 1 Osteoarthritis; Larry Lytle

The Power of Now, A guide to Spiritual Enlightenment; Eckhart Tolle, New World Library, Novato,CA

Nervous System and Sensory Organs – a Color Atlas /Text of Human Anatomy, vol 3; Werner Kahle, Thieme Medical Publishers, New York

Anatomy of an Illness, Norman Cousins, Norton and Company, 1979, New York

Origin of the Universe and the Secret of Light and Magnetism, E.Y. Webb 1949, Republished 1993, Mark Foster, Bountiful, UT

Psycho-Cybernetics, Maxwell Maltz, Prentice Hall 1950, Republished 1973, Pocket Books, New York

Energy Medicine, Donna Eden, Penguin Putman, New York 1998

Vibrational Medicine, the #1 Handbook of Subtle-Energy Therapies, Richard Gerber, Bear & Co, 3rd ed. 1954

No Ordinary Moments, Dan Millman, New world Library, 1992

Printed in the United States
95892LV00005B/1-15/A